# IN THE FORESTS OF THE NIGHT

*Frontispiece*

GIANT FOREST HOG—This picture was taken at a distance of four to five feet as the animal was charging the camera. The blinding light of the flashbulb made him swerve off to the right.

# In the Forests of the Night

JAMES RIDDELL

LONDON
ROBERT HALE LIMITED
18 Bedford Square W.C.1
1948

# INTRODUCTION

This book should have been written by Gander.

His full name was Kenneth Cecil Gandar Dower—but everyone knew him as Gander . . . and it is to his memory that this book is dedicated.

He was a person to whom travel and adventure were the essence of living, and, during his life, he made adventure out of most things, even out of the smallest and most commonplace event or journey. I can remember many a day spent in his company, clambering over rocks at the seaside, or wading about in a fen in the rain in Cambridgeshire, or canoeing down the upper reaches of the Thames, or even climbing trees in Ashridge Park, which he somehow managed to turn into days of high adventure.

He loved Africa with a very great love because, even in these days when all of it is known and explored, it was a place that still stood for Adventure.

He had very many facets. He was one of the best allround ball-games players that England has ever produced. He had a fine brain and one of the most retentive memories you could wish to find. He spoke well in public and those who have read his books will know that he had a great future as an author. But best of all, he had a wonderful sense of humor. He could laugh at the world and with the world, but the best joke of the lot was himself.

He was a very good friend—

I repeat, he should have written this book.

W. J. R.

# CONTENTS

# LIST OF ILLUSTRATIONS

Charts and Illustrations drawn by the Author

Page

# IN THE FORESTS OF THE NIGHT

# CHAPTER I: THE EXCUSE

There was a time when it was considered that young men who suddenly left England for a year and headed for the back of beyond for no other purpose than to explore places and shoot things, could only be excused as being either eccentric or badly crossed in love—or both.

When we set out from England in 1938 we could only lay modest claims to the former of these.

It seems that the more eccentric or the more disastrously crossed in love you happened to be, the more remote the place or the harder the task you chose. Well . . . we set out for a place which, as far as I was concerned, seemed even behind the back of beyond, and we set ourselves a task that appeared to me to range ridiculously close to the impossible—so, by all rights and reasons, I, at least, should have been most terribly crossed in love. But, as I have said, this wasn't quite the case.

Finally, in those good days, when the traveller returned, healed of heart or empty of pocket (and probably both) he found himself lionized by audiences who, geographically anyway, had only the very vaguest idea of where he had actually

Our excuse for going to Africa was to take pictures of animals. . . .

been. The beauty of the thing was that there was seldom anybody qualified to question the authenticity of his tales, and in lecture halls or at dinner parties he used to be able to get away with murder. . . .

This, I can state categorically, was not the case with us.

To begin with, we didn't return. Gander never returned. The ship in which he was traveling to the Far East in 1942 was torpedoed off Ceylon, and he was drowned. I only returned six years after leaving—and when I did I found that both for myself and for countless others, the back of beyond had somehow ceased to be, and that the world had shrunk.

In the England I had left in 1938 men talked, in terms of travel, of Blackpool, and Brighton, and the braver of Boulogne. Now, in the trains and pubs and queues, it is Beirut, Burma, Balikpapan and beyond.

The back of beyond as we knew it has gone . . . and so, very largely, have the standards of difficult tasks that a man may set himself to accomplish, for there is nothing that I can think of to compare with some of the many "impossibles" achieved during the war.

There is now a new kind of "back of beyond." It has moved over, with alarming suddenness, from the geographical into the realm of the scientist and chemist—and already the curtain is beginning to be drawn aside. I find now, with a certain amount of sadness, that when the talk follows the line of modern adventure and discovery, when energy is atomic, and propulsion is by reaction, and travel is in the region of the speed of sound—and everything is neutrons, and plastics and uranium and jets—that the flood of words quickly goes over my head, and I am out of my depth.

The old "Back of Beyond" which the white man conquered by exploration and travel and adventure will not properly return until the white man has blown himself to atoms or traveled off in mass to distant planets. Then it will come back

—when the black man, the native of central New Guinea, and the pigmy from the Ituri Forest will wonder what has happened and will sally forth with trepidation (and who shall blame him?) to discover the lands where once the white man lived.

* * *

I forget exactly when we decided to go. We had wanted to go for a long time but I think it came to a head more or less immediately after Munich when Chamberlain came back with "Peace in our time." It was partly to escape from the "Peace" that followed, and partly because we both wanted to do something interesting and adventurous before the inevitable happened, while we yet had time.

We had often discussed where we should go and what we should do when we got there, and we spent many an evening lying on the floor poring over maps of the world. Maps always have a stimulating effect. They quickly convert the simplest of ideas into highly ambitious schemes. We found ourselves going to most places on those maps. We penetrated the worst parts of Brazil. . . . We climbed the Mountains of the Moon and wandered in the forests of the Belgian Congo. . . . We even got an aeroplane and dropped supplies to ourselves on Mount Wilhelminatop in Dutch New Guinea. . . . We went almost everywhere, and it was always fun.

So it was that our plans gradually did become more and more ambitious, and as they did so, of course, more and more snags arose. But eventually, after making many contacts and writing many letters, and flying to Brussels and back, the choice fell on the Belgian Congo—and we were settled. The aim of the expedition was to be photography; the subjects for the cameras, animals; the final objective, the Gorilla.

I suppose it is strange that two people should choose to travel so far to take a photograph of a gorilla, when the

. . . and to take photographs of Africa . . . THOMSON'S FALLS KENYA
(*picture by moonlight—29 minute exposure.*)

. . . and to find out what Equatorial Africa was all about. . . .
LAKE KIVU, BELGIAN CONGO (*looking west across lake.*)

whole job could, at that time, have been done quite easily by taking a bus to Regent's Park and pointing a camera through the bars at Mok and Moina in the London Zoo. Unfortunately, even this is impossible now, as they are dead. But although plenty of pictures of complacent gorillas sitting about in uncomfortable cages do exist, the stimulus lay in the fact that there are very few photographs of gorillas at large in their natural home and surroundings—where, as I now know, they are anything but complacent.

One or two people have succeeded in getting the real thing in the forests of the Congo, but the pictures they produced are dim, because the great ape lives in very dense country where, generally speaking, the light is insufficient for anything really satisfactory in the way of a photograph.

In any case it was an excuse for adventure. That was all we wanted. Besides this, there were several other animals that had never been photographed at all.

* * *

# CHAPTER II: THE VOYAGE

One's friends were not helpful, they were plainly discouraging. "You'll get," they said, "yellow fever and blackwater, and you'll have a dismal time in swamps . . . " I didn't at all. I got phlebitis and dysentery, and had a dismal time in forests, and I'm glad I proved our friends wrong because I wouldn't have missed one minute of it for all the tea in China.

"With all those elephants and gorillas and snakes around," they said, "you'll be simply scared to death . . . " There they were on safer ground, but they were wrong again . . . it wasn't to death that I was scared—only at times into extreme liveliness.

"Or are you going," they said, unfairly this time, "merely to prove how brave you are?" And here I am happy to state that they were utterly wrong, for if I proved anything to myself, it was on several occasions how very frightened I could be.

We had what I hope, was a very unusual voyage. We set sail from Marseilles in a ship whose name I am not prepared to advertise, for she belonged to a famous line. She must in any case have been pensioned off before September 1939, for

. . . we wanted to live and move around in the fantastic forests of the Congo. . . . FOREST SCENE, MOUNT MIKENO, BELGIAN CONGO—(*taken at approximately 13,000 feet.*)

. . . and see and hear and feel the strange insistent rhythm of Africa. DANCER AT WATUSSI CELEBRATIONS: KIGALE, RUANDA URUNDI.

This was the kind of photograph we planned to take. . . .
LEOPARD IN THE ABERDARE MOUNTAINS, KENYA.

if on wartime voyages she had been forced to zig-zag as well, she would never have got anywhere at all. And so, for a not too modest sum, we were gradually transported to East Africa. The company admitted that it was unfortunate that we had to travel in this ship, as she was old and that this was her last voyage before being broken up. She was old all right, but we subsequently found that they had been saying this to passengers for the last ten voyages at least—and in any case the ship required little in the way of breaking up. . . . I suspect that one good sudden burst on the siren would have done the trick.

We seemed to call in at every port we could, and every time we did we arrived late and left late, and the crew could hardly be blamed for going ashore as often as was possible. Members of this crew were always arriving back in the middle of the night in that wide-open state of happiness that is of great entertainment to the party-minded and of low diversionary value to the sleeper in his bunk. And even though our departures were invariably late, we always seemed to be leaving one or two behind.

While we were on the move, the deck, wherever you seemed to be sitting, was bathed in a surprisingly steady rain of soot and the further we went the deeper the layer of soot grew and lay underfoot. It seems that it was not practicable to be too lavish with the water when hosing down the decks in the morning as the decks themselves were leaky and water was apt to go unhindered into the cabins below.

Memories of our fellow passengers in the Tourist Class fade compared with those of the twenty-eight missionaries. . . . On voyages of this nature a missionary or two is to be expected, but a gaggle of twenty-eight is something one rarely encounters. They mostly wore black, so the soot was not really so very noticeable, but it was a little like being locked up in the coal cellar with the vicar for weeks on end.

. . . and this is what often happened to the best laid plans. In this case we were expecting an animal of reasonable proportions—but an elephant came by instead.

We hoped at least that we would look the part. . . . Safari Boys and Author, Belgian Congo.

Travel with Gander, however, was seldom dull. We had some evenings I shall not forget, converting the missionaries.

Yes—it was an unusual trip. . . . However, we travelled hopefully, and furthermore, we arrived.

The train journey from Mombasa to Nairobi has been done by countless thousands of people, but to me it was new and everything was intensely interesting. It was my first sight of Africa and my first introduction to the equator, and impressions and surprises came thick and fast. The people, the villages, the trees and flowers, the butterflies, the landscape, the feeling of vastness, the very smell of the sunshine and the earth that is somehow Africa, all these things and many more were new and thrilling to this Londoner that I am.

I know that is badly put—the sunshine doesn't smell—but there is some scent about Africa, you could even sense it from the sea before land was sighted, that is connected with sunshine and earth and things primitive and strange and exciting, and I fear I cannot put it better.

The sun went down that evening in spectacular fashion and there was a flaming, fiery effect in a sky that somehow seemed enormously bigger than the skies in England. I went to bed in the sleeping car with a great impatience for the next day, and with a great thankfulness for having come to Africa.

The next morning at breakfast the train was running through what appeared to be a Whipsnade Zoo of gargantuan proportions. Wildebeeste, ostrich, gazelle, impala, giraffe, Secretary bird, vulture, zebra. . . . So much to look at that the coffee on the table grew cold.

Then came Nairobi—and plans to be made for the first trials of our schemes in the wild and beautiful country that can be found quite close to the capital town of Kenya Colony.

* * *

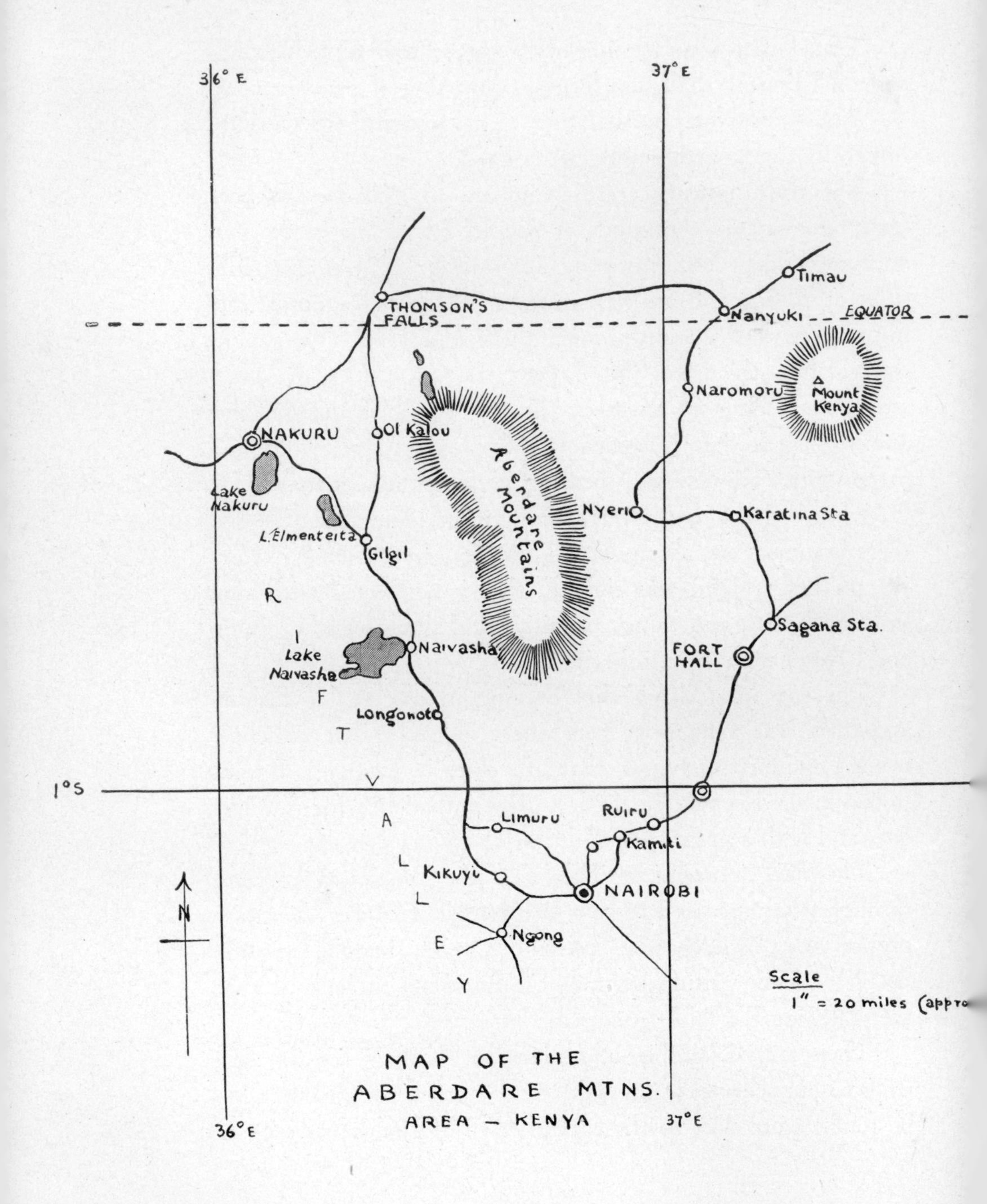
36° E
37° E
THOMSON'S FALLS
Timau
Nanyuki
EQUATOR
Mount Kenya
Naromoru
NAKURU
Ol Kalou
Aberdare Mountains
Lake Nakuru
Nyeri
Karatina Sta
L. Elmenteita
Gilgil
R I F T V A L L E Y
Lake Naivasha
Naivasha
Sagana Sta.
FORT HALL
Longonot
1° S
Limuru
Ruiru
Kamiti
Kikuyu
NAIROBI
Ngong
N
Scale
1" = 20 miles (appro
MAP OF THE ABERDARE MTNS. AREA — KENYA
36° E
37° E

# CHAPTER III: THE SCHEME

Before I go any further I should like to get it off my chest that although we made close contact with gorillas—far too close for my liking—we never succeeded in getting a satisfactory picture of one, and no gorilla photograph appears in this book. If anything, this was really the gorilla's fault—he was the one who was unco-operative. He, and Hitler. If Hitler had only decided to liberate Poland two weeks later we should have done the trick. I am convinced of this, for we had made plans which I don't think would have failed—but I will tell of those later.

It was never our intention to travel all that way to get one or two pictures of one or two animals. We were no purists. I have to admit that while, on the one hand, we wanted the fun and the adventure, on the other we were certainly not blind to the commercial side of things. We wanted lots of pictures of lots of animals . . . good sellable pictures of a kind that could at least return some of the expenses involved and possibly event show a profit.

As a point of interest you do not necessarily have to be

NJOKI—Who was batman, cook and general bottle washer to us both.

a millionaire to do these things. If you want to, you can make an expedition to the Congo cost a small fortune. Taking into consideration the distances and the time involved, and the equipment necessary and everything, a year's expedition of this nature, properly handled and modestly carried out, can be made to cost approximately the same as it would have done for Gander and me to share in buying a new Rolls-Royce. On top of this there seemed every good possibility of doing the equivalent to getting a reasonable second-hand price for the Rolls-Royce after using it for a year.

Nevertheless we hardly thought in terms of showing a profit. We had made a little money out of two books we had written together and we felt like spending it as well as we could. So we did this, and merely hoped that a little of it might one day come back. One of the main snags to making the expedition pay at all lay in the fact that although we had done a good deal of amateur photography, neither Gander nor I could consider ourselves in any way professionals. We had a lot to learn, and before we left England we learned as much as we could.

Now even to the meanest intelligence it quickly becomes plain that the two of us creeping around in orthodox fashion in the dark Congo forests, each one with a single camera, however much at the ready, might well have to creep around for a very long time before any animal, let alone a gorilla, would become sufficiently convinced of our integrity and commercial ambitions to stand and pose for us.

We got out of that difficulty by buying twenty cameras.

As soon as this became known to our friends the old question of carrying eccentricity one step too far came up again.

We continued to show our determination by buying twenty Burvin Synchronisers, a large quantity of film, a thousand Phillips' Flash Bulbs, countless gadgets, a pair of shorts each and two very impressive topees. After this the question of eccentricity was dropped altogether. We did not tell anybody that the cameras were second-and third-hand and that we got a reduction for quantity. They were Leica cameras, but you must remember that in those days Leicas were not made out of platinum, as they apparently are to-day.

As soon as we got to Nairobi, along with our great coffins of photographic equipment, we found ourselves subjected to the same kind of frivolous comment we had weathered in England. Here, however, we were up against "people who knew what they were talking about," and we found ourselves treated very largely as figures of fun. But the people of Nairobi are as friendly a bunch of people as I have ever met, and we were also treated with great hospitality and friendliness and given a lot of very valuable help. And, come to think of it, nobody has more fun than a figure of fun.

So, in accordance with our schemes, we continued our orgy of buying. We bought axes, pangas,* miles of string and rolls of cotton, scissors, nails, wooden stakes, clamps, chicken wire, tape measures, reflectors, batteries, wire, screws, soft-soap, dusters, lens-heads and a hundred and one other odds and ends which were all to have their uses. We also hired from the firm of Safarilands Ltd., a tent with a double fly and what we considered complete camping equipment to go with it. Safarilands was more accustomed to dealing with rich Americans and Royalty than with people like us, and I often suspected them of being more than merely amused. . . . For transport we hired first a large station wagon Ford V-8 and, as soon as we had completed our purchases we found we had to add a ton and a half truck, also a Ford, as well. And finally, as soon as we held our first loading exercise to see if we could get all our kit on board we found that it was necessary to build a great cage-like

* *Machetes, or long bladed knives.*

construction on top of the open truck to hold everything on. When it was completed it was an impressive sight—it looked as though we were going in for transporting giraffes from one place to another.

Those final days, before setting out for the first trial of our equipment, were hectic indeed. The days seemed too short for all the things we had to do, and we didn't get much sleep at night, because Nairobi is apt to be gay.

For our first experiments we required a subject on which to see how well or how badly our photographic scheme would work—just one of the many animals of Africa—one that would, so to speak, play ball with us—but not too roughly.

We could of course have tried it out on the dog. There was a dog quite handy in Jim and Rachael's house where we were staying, an ugly and impossibly sentimental bull-terrier named "Pickle," but somehow we felt we hadn't come all that way to play around with bull-terriers. Besides this, "Weary" Wood, our guide and counsellor at Kodaks in Nairobi, would have dined out on the story of the first results of the Dower-Riddell Big Game Expedition for weeks to come.

In the end Gander selected the hippopotamus to be our first victim—and immediately and quite frankly I told him I thought this was unnecessarily advanced. I could have thought of many lesser animals more likely to play ball with us than a hippo. What I had in mind was something smaller and more likely to be a little scared of me, like, . . . well, . . . say a gazelle, or possibly a zebra . . . But I would have been wrong; I might have been weeks before having success with either of them.

The hippo, it was pointed out, is far more a creature of habit than the gregarious and timid animals of the plains and therefore his movements are more predictable. He is not, and this I could easily understand, scared of anything in particular. And finally he does not wander far from the place in which he lives and, in spite of his appearance, is relatively harmless. The last part of this description could at one time, I found, have equally well applied to myself, but I was unconvinced that I and the hippopotamus had anything at all in common. The only one warning that I was given, in order not to provoke this large and heavy animal, was to avoid getting between him and water. In theory this was sound, but in practice, wherever hippos are, there seems always to be water on every hand.

However, we went—car, lorry, equipment and all—to a place where hippos lived. With us were the two "Boys" we had taken on to our strength in Nairobi. They stayed with us, surprisingly, for the whole of our time in Africa and they shared with us our way of living, our triumphs, and our various humiliations. Jepharia was the driver of the truck. He had, of course, a naturally dark countenance, which was, however ludicrous a situation, seldom lightened by a smile. Njoki was batman, cook and general bottle-washer to us both. He had an even darker countenance which, more often than not, was positively flood-lit by the broadest of African grins, in which a perfect set of teeth played the part of neon lights. I could always find Njoki in the dark by just looking round for a set of teeth.

Speaking of the dark reminds me that I haven't yet explained the manner in which we intended to take our pictures. All animal photography was to be done at night. It was reasonable to suppose that night-time would be the time least expected by any animal to find people about with cameras, and in consequence he would be undisturbed and natural. Most pictures I have seen of African animals have been taken by daylight and they show that the animal is well aware of a disturbance nearby.

The first job was to locate the animal or animals we wanted, watch them and study their movements as closely as possible,

We went to a place where the Hippos lived. . . . Lake Naivasha.

and then set photographic traps for them. We figured that with twenty cameras we could cover quite a large area and allow for latitude of movement and choice of routes on the part of the animals concerned. Using so many cameras, spread out over so much ground made it impossible to use the normal method of leaving the shutter open and having a trip-wire merely release the flash-bulb. There would not have been time to get round to all the cameras last thing at night to open them, and again before first light to close them, and the films would have been spoiled. Africa is also subject to thunder storms of considerable intensity, and lightning would blur the film. In any case there are limits to the amount of wandering around at night that you can do in Africa. . . .

So we had to have a contrivance that would, on being tripped, release both shutter and flash-bulb simultaneously. This, with minor home made modifications, we did with the Burvin Synchroniser, a device which fitted on to the bottom of the Leica cameras. But even with this excellent gadget the timing and tripping was more than tricky. Roughly the sequence of setting a camera trap is as follows:

First you select a spot where you hope the animal in question will pass by to within a few inches. You then select a suitable place for the camera where it can "see" and yet is itself not too obvious. A flash bulb only has a limited field of lighting efficiency and, of course, the further away from the subject you place the camera the slower you must make your shutter speed—and the more you do this the less likely you are to get a picture free of movement and consequent blur. In general we found that twenty-four feet was about the maximum, and most of our pictures were taken well inside this range. Having selected the two sites, one for the camera and one for the animal, you have to find some means for firmly securing the camera in the required position. This we did with strong metal spring clamps which we fastened either to tree trunks or to stakes driven into the ground. The next step is to ensure correct focus, and further than that, correct depth of focus—with the subject for the picture conspicuous by its absence. It became fairly general practice for one of us to cope with the setting and angling of the camera while the other impersonated the animal. As soon as Njoki understood the full import of this strange behaviour he became a willing "animal" and saved a lot of loss of dignity. Depth of focus, of course, varied considerably according to which animal we were expecting. What was right for a leopard was wrong for an elephant or a mongoose, and each time variations to the shutter aperture were necessary they had to be related to shutter-speed, distance and flash-bulb.

So it is understandable that there were plenty of controversial things for two people to discuss.

Next the camera has to be protected from the weather and camouflaged and hidden as well as possible. This was done by means of tin boxes, chicken wire, moss and general foliage. Camouflage, however, must not be done too wholeheartedly as it soon becomes impossible to reach the camera to make adjustments, and furthermore, if twenty cameras spread over a large area of thick country are too cunningly concealed, they become incredibly difficult to find the next day. We always had in any case to make fairly detailed charts of all areas giving exact locations.

I remember one day Gander's voice came floating down from the top of a small hill nearby.

"Where the hell did you put the camera up on this hill, Jimmy?"

"Who's making a noise now?" I shouted back.

"Well . . . where is it anyway?"

"Right by the big tree on the left of the track—but mind the trip wire—that's this side of the tree." A long pause

One tiny sound can startle the animal and ruin the picture.
GAZELLE.

followed this and I went on with my work, mending a mechanism. Presently . . .

"There are lots of big trees up here and I'm damned if I can see it. You come up and show me."

With a show of some reluctance, I set down the synchroniser and toiled up the track. It was very hot.

"You must be as blind as a bat," I said when I joined him, "it's right there under your nose," and I marched confidently right up to where I had set the camera. There was a blinding flash from the right hand side of the track opposite the tree as I walked straight into the trip-wire. . . . I stood quite still for a moment.

"Thank you," said Gander, "I knew you'd find it for me," and when I was halfway down the hill again he added, "We needed a flashlight picture of you looking pompous anyway. . . ."

The trigger release that sets off shutter and flash-bulb requires a setting that will allow it to work at the slightest touch on the trip-wire, so that a picture can be taken before any warning clicks or sounds can come from the apparatus. One tiny sound, however insignificant normally, can startle the animal and ruin the picture.

For trip-wires we used black cotton. The fact that an elephant, lumbering into a strand of black cotton stretched across a path can take his own photograph in the fractional interval between touching *and breaking* the cotton, shows how delicately the trigger release has to be set. (It has, furthermore, to work equally well for the lightest and sprightliest animals.) It also becomes evident that to get the "pull" transferred directly to the camera trigger the trip-wire must "run" absolutely free. Cotton does not "run" freely round tree-trunks —it catches and breaks. We had therefore to knock in bent nails at every point where the cotton led at an angle to the actual trip-wire.

The setting of the trip-wires themselves presents no small problem. Apart from the layout of the trap itself, you have to try to ensure that no animal is likely to pass through and touch off the cotton that leads from the camera to the trip-wire. This can only result in an out-of-focus close-up. It can be avoided in various ways according to the site selected, but generally it is best done by putting it high.

Again, animal traffic along the game trails and paths is not, unfortunately, a tidy affair where the lion sticks to one path and the bush buck to another. The height, however, at which the trip-wire is set can, to a certain extent, select required subjects. A cotton stretched across a trail at a height of five feet can catch the buffalo or eland and allow the leopard or gazelle to pass below—but if you are after the tiny dik-dik with the cotton stretched a few inches off the ground you are just as likely to get a close-up of an elephant foot.

Gander once spent a great deal of time and energy on a very tricky little job of getting a close-up of some very small animal. It was all a matter of inches, with a trip-wire practically lying on the ground. He had a method all his own of setting cameras by getting right down and peering into the camera to see if the lens was pointing in the right direction. Sooner or later the inevitable occurred and a very anxious-looking and sweaty face took its own photograph in the blinding light of the flash-bulb. I'm afraid I couldn't resist the remark that on the whole it was a good thing because it would save us the trouble of getting a baboon.

Later on this same camera took an excellent portrait of an elephant's foot, with just the tip of the trunk thrown in for good measure.

I hesitate to go further into technicalities or into the ramifications of the many Rube Goldberg devices that we employed, for fear of becoming a bore. The initial problems, however, which, on paper, we knew we had to solve were as nothing

Sometimes they came too close and touched off the connection that led from camera to trip wire. ELAND

compared with the problems that arose as we went along. I hope I have made it clear that the process was reasonably complicated, because it undoubtedly was—and as things had to be done with the maximum speed and the minimum noise, since we were nearly always working with animals of various sorts and sizes in the vicinity, the reader may perhaps be able to visualize some of the situations that arose.

The whole business of setting a camera, let alone twenty, was one of those things that is liable to make two people either extremely cross with one another, or have them both weak with laughter.

* * *

NUTRIA—imported into Kenya from the Argentina.

Never get between him and the water.

# CHAPTER IV: THE TRIAL

The place where the hippos lived was ideal for first experiments. They lived in a relatively undisturbed corner of a lake where, for a distance of about a mile along the lake shore the ground bore lots of evidence of hippo spoor coming and going between the water and the papyrus. This papyrus, which is simply tall reeds ten to fifteen feet high, grew thickly in the mud and swampland at the corner of the lake and covered an area of several acres. The hippos spent their time between the lake and the papyrus and in moving about in the latter they had created a complicated series of tunnels, much on the lines of the London Underground railway system, through which one could crawl and wade. It was an exciting place that papyrus, and one where it was relatively easy to predict exactly where the hippo would go. It was also a place from which, once you were well inside and crawling along in the tunnels, there was no escape. It was, too, extremely easy to get yourself as well and truly lost as in a maze.

You could always hear the hippos snorting and blowing, sometimes close to you and sometimes nicely distant. I always

Bush Pig—Sometimes various animals would come by before nightfall and help themselves to a picture. In this case the leading animal was curious about the small stone to which the cotton trip wire was attached.

had the feeling that round every corner I would come face to face with one travelling in the opposite direction. Face to face with a hippo in a tunnel at a distance of a few feet is an unenviable position in which to find oneself—and as far as faces are concerned the hippo has the advantage. Or worse still, I couldn't help at times suspecting that a hippo had come into my tunnel behind me, down a branch line, and was following along and blocking my exit—and, if anything, hippos just behind you in tunnels are strategically better placed than just in front.

I often wonder exactly what I, with a camera in one hand and a wooden stake in the other, or the hippo with nothing at all to encumber him, would have done had such an emergency arisen. I suspect there would certainly have been a stupid misunderstanding.

We found, during the course of the first day, that hippos were not the only inhabitants of this particular corner of Kenya. We saw bushpig, impala, waterbuck, jackall, ostrich, duiker and the spoor of many more, including leopard.

We set cameras both inside and outside the papyrus and we found, inexperienced as we were, that it took incredibly long to set even one trap. During the whole of the first day's work we only managed to set three cameras, and we retired that evening, well after dark, tired, badly bitten by mosquitos, and just a little bit dispirited.

The following morning was rather like that moment at a depressing party when the door opens and somebody walks in with a trayful of drinks. With mounting excitement we went to each of the three cameras and found that all of them had worked! The tell-tale, grey, opaque colour of the flash-bulbs, the broken trip-wires, the fresh spoor in the mud—everything was there as we had planned. . . . It was a great moment.

Excitedly we fell to examining the ground at each of the sites, and, neither of us being very expert as yet at interpreting

Unintentional Photography—Various tense and undignified attitudes.

spoor, our joint conjectures sounded rather as though Noah had beached the Ark during the night on the lake-shore and that everything in it had walked obediently through our traps.

In the end we decided that the three cameras had succeeded with hippo, leopard and some kind of antelope respectively. In any case we were sure we had results.

We quickly reset these cameras and during the rest of the day, by dint of working like blacks (and by somehow persuading our two blacks to work like us) we managed to put up five more camera traps. In our hurry we also managed to get ourselves inextricably entangled in yards and yards of black cotton and we took several unexpected photographs of ourselves in various tense and undignified attitudes.

"If it goes on like this," said Gander at one point, just after I had taken an unnecessary picture of the back of his pants, "we may have to revise the whole expedition. We might even find it better to hand the whole thing over to the animals and have them take a series of intimate shots of white men at work. . . . "

During that day I was an interested spectator at what subsequently turned out to be the amorous advances of one hippo to another. At the outset it looked like the beginning of a first class family row. Mrs. Hippo, at least I can only presume and hope it was Mrs. Hippo, stood coyly about in some bushes some ten or twenty yards from the lake. Romeo, heavily disguised as Mr. Hippo, after a period of keen circling, approached his Juliet at a steady rate of some five to seven knots and, with resounding impact, barged the whole of his great bulk straight into Mrs. Hippo's flank. This heavy collision evidently gave both of them considerable satisfaction, for it was repeated several times from almost every angle of approach until the area where they were began to have every appearance of a battlefield, and most of the bushes were laid waste.

To a reasonably normal human being, devoid of any outstanding fetichisms, it looked for all the world like deliberate provocation to a stand-up fight, but this was far from the case, for presently the two of them went off happily together, hand in hand as it were, down into the water. And there, having drawn a more or less discreet and watery curtain over their activities, it was only to be supposed that they got down to the real business of the day, for a series of minor and rhythmical tidal waves started to roll up on the shore.

The next day four out of the seven cameras had worked perfectly. This time we finally interpreted our bag as otter, dik-dik, another hippo, and, strangely enough, python. We had set one trip-line right at the water's edge, half in the water and half in the mud, and there right across it, broken cotton and all, was the unmistakable trail of a fairly large snake.

The next day, and the next, rewarded us with much the same number of results.

We stayed by that lake-shore for approximately a week. By the end of that time we had counted some twenty successful "trips," and we were impatient to have the films developed to see the quality of our results—so we packed everything up and departed back to Nairobi. This impatience was quite natural and genuine, although it may possibly have been accelerated slightly by a discovery we made that morning.

We were crawling along one of the tunnels when we came across the impressive, and very fresh, spoor of lion. . . . Lions in the open are one thing—lions in restricted tunnels are quite another.

We easily convinced ourselves that the results of photography were of paramount importance, and that lions could wait to have their pictures taken at some later date. After all, there were plenty of lions in Africa, and only two of us.

Once back in Nairobi we found a lot of mail waiting for us. It appeared from several telegrams we received that a certain amount of chaos was reigning back at home in England over our joint affairs. This was, on the whole, not so very unusual, but this time it seemed a bit more important. Before leaving England we had written a revue together—and Michael North of B.B.C. fame had produced excellent music to our lyrics. It was a nonsensical political satire affair called "Grave New World", and we had left it in the hands of agents, with friends acting on our behalf. These telegrams told us that it had been accepted and that production in London at some not-too-distant date was intended; but the trouble was, although I forget exactly why, we were both required back in London at once to cope with things.

This was exciting and disturbing news. By now we were both badly bitten by our new occupation and the last thing we wanted to do was to leave Africa—so, after a long discussion, we sent off a three page cable saying we were both very sorry but that we were quite sure that negotiations and general arrangements would inevitably go more smoothly if we ourselves were absent — meanwhile we were off to the Congo — goodbye.

It was a difficult decision to make because—well, because . . . but I'm sure we were right—and anyway, in the end our unfortunate revue was just another of the many things that Hitler was responsible for stopping. . . .

It was with very mingled feelings on the following day that we came out of Kodaks having inspected the negatives of our pictures. We had been expecting twenty results . . . we got four. Of these, three could just be called satisfactory—and only one was really good. The remainder were washouts.

Gander and I were both bitterly disappointed with this meager return for a whole week's work. We were soon to know better . . . but somehow or other we never seemed to manage to

When you arrange for Hippos to come out of a lake and face the camera they have a maddening habit of doing the very reverse. . . .

This one, with a strange overgrown tusk, did precisely the same.

stay miserable for very long—and, after all, there was that one grand picture. It was a hippo, three-quarter front view, just about to indulge in a dust bath. We had found the place together and seen that hippos went there just for that purpose, but, in a generous session of mutual commiseration over the other failures, each one congratulated the other on his cleverness in finding the site and the brilliance of setting of the trap—and soon, enthusiasm, like a resilient rubber ball, was bouncing again.

The three pictures that were only just satisfactory were largely so because the animals were too far away and had apparently chosen to go through our trip-wires backwards—and, however hard you try, it is difficult to make an attractive picture out of the wrong end of a hippo. . . . This, however, could easily be overcome by more cunning arrangement of the trip-wires.

And then we got down to a thorough analysis of the sixteen or so washouts. Among these there were several very excellent photographs of papyrus and bushes and undergrowth, but with nothing whatsoever in the way of an animal in the picture—this we found was due to the cotton trip-wire being stretched too taut between the stems of the papyrus, and the wind, blowing the reeds about, had set off the triggers.

One or two similar pictures of nothing but vegetation had small blurs across the centre of the negatives—there is little you can do to prevent birds flying through cotton trip-wires. Others were badly blurred—rain and condensation on the lens. (This was to prove a constant problem all along.) There were one or two negatives on which the vague outlines of animals were discernible, but it was very much a matter of 'through a glass darkly'—these were plainly cases of poor synchronisation of shutter and flash-bulb. And finally, there was one slap-up picture of Njoki trying, and failing, to step over a trip-wire.

Snags. (1) There is little you can do to prevent birds flying through cotton trip wires. . . .

(11) Evidence of an unreported event. . . .

He looked very sheepish when we confronted him with this evidence of an unreported event. . . .

But the main thing was—it worked.

The next thing was to try it out in the forests of the Aberdare Mountains.

* * *

THE CHANIA RIVER, ABERDARE MOUNTAINS.

Some of the forest creatures appeared to have come straight out of a Disney film. BUSH BUCK.

# CHAPTER V: THE FOREST

As I look back down the crowded distances of the last six years I find I am no longer interested in an exact chronicle of where we went next or of all the many things we did in Africa and the order in which we did them—and I am convinced that a straightforward diary would find the reader even less interested than I. . . . This, after all, is a book of pictures, and there is little enough excuse for writing anything at all. But it is difficult, in the kaleidoscope of jumbled memories of one of the happiest and most interesting periods of my life, to know which moments to pull out and do my best to describe.

We went to the Aberdare Mountains for two main reasons. First, because our photographic system was, as yet, far from perfect and needed considerable practice, and second, because we wanted to do that practice in the same kind of conditions we were going to meet in the Congo forests.

On our various trips we never took a white hunter with us—and only on one occasion a rifle. This was not mere foolish bravado. It may have been a little foolish and it's true that a spot of bravado may have slipped in somewhere, but the real reason was that we wanted, as nearly as possible, to be on level terms with the animals. Even the whitest of white hunters cannot cease to feel a sense of responsibility for his clients and he cannot help but be a restraining influence. As to the matter of weapons, at that time I would probably have been in greater danger with a rifle than without, and in any case in the Reserves of the Congo, our eventual destination, arms were not allowed, so it seemed reasonable to become accustomed to being unarmed from the start.

We had no intention whatsoever of harming any animal and we hoped very sincerely that the animals would see our point of view and not harm us.

From the outside, viewed across the wide expanse of the Great Rift Valley, the Aberdare Mountains are not impressive. The range works itself up to its highest point—Mount Kinangop, 12,800 ft.—so gradually that it appears to be quite an insignificant line of hills. From the inside, however, once you are in there in the forests, the Aberdares are decidedly impressive. Surrounded as they are, on every hand, by civilization they cannot possibly be called "off the map"—and yet, once you get inside, you are, to all intents and purposes, way off any map.

The site we chose for our base camp was in the middle of the "Bamboo Belt." We got there, after the usual false alarms and curious excursions, by driving our miniature convoy as far up as we could (and that was a good deal farther than most normal people would have taken cars) and then by employing fifteen porters. . . .

The moment I got inside those forests I was lost—utterly, completely and bewilderingly lost. The whole world consisted of bamboos—thousands upon thousands upon thousands of bamboos. They stood close together in solid phalanx like a nightmare maze of poles. Some fifteen feet up the feathery fronds formed a roof overhead—and over that again there was an-

The moment I got inside that forest I was lost. BAMBOO FORESTS, ABERDARE MOUNTAINS.

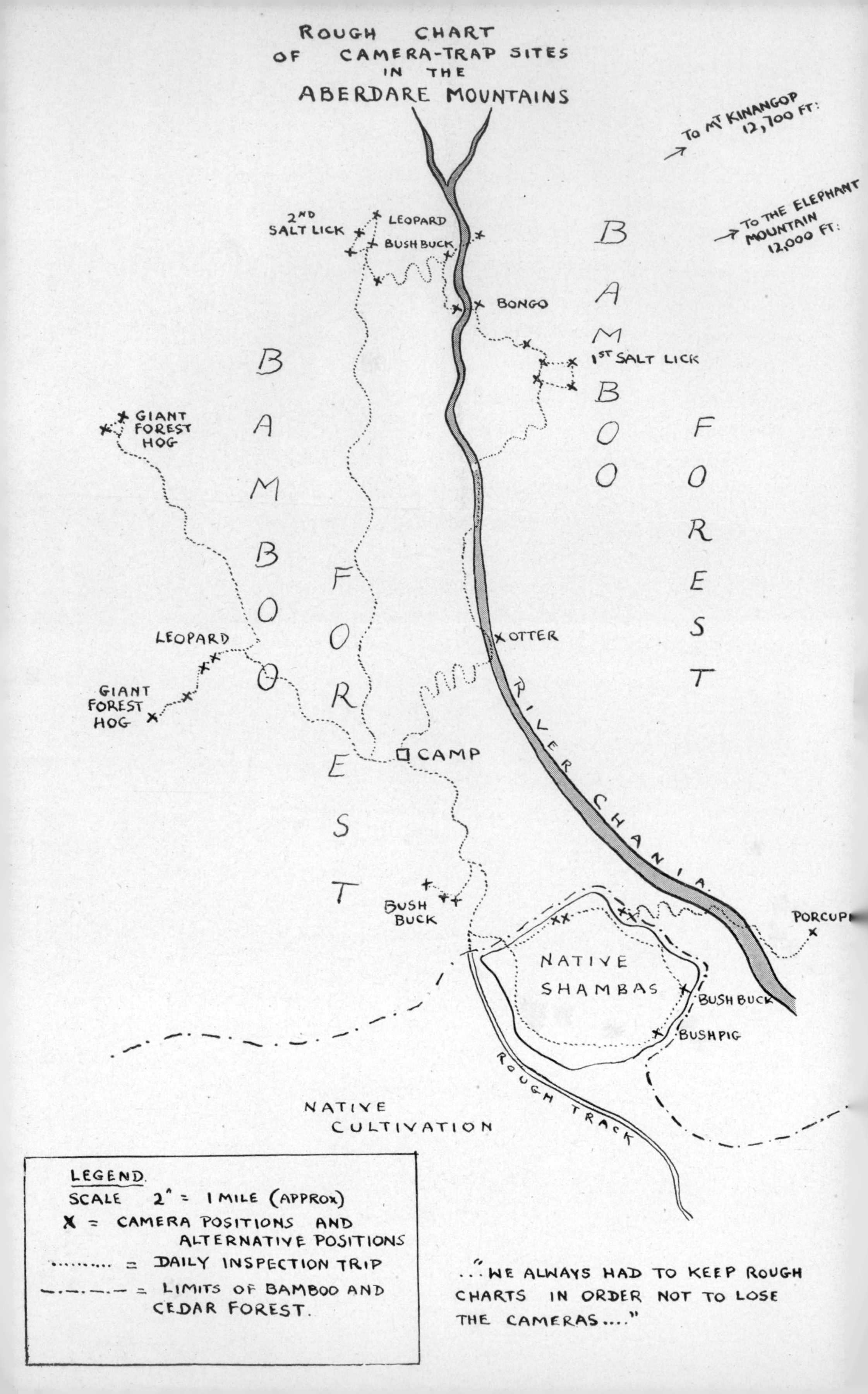
ROUGH CHART
OF CAMERA-TRAP SITES
IN THE
ABERDARE MOUNTAINS
TO MT KINANGOP 12,700 FT:
TO THE ELEPHANT MOUNTAIN 12,000 FT:
2ND SALT LICK
LEOPARD
BUSHBUCK
BONGO
1ST SALT LICK
BAMBOO FOREST
BAMBOO FOREST
GIANT FOREST HOG
LEOPARD
GIANT FOREST HOG
OTTER
RIVER CHANIA
CAMP
BUSH BUCK
PORCUP
NATIVE SHAMBAS
BUSHBUCK
BUSHPIG
ROUGH TRACK
NATIVE CULTIVATION
LEGEND.
SCALE 2" = 1 MILE (APPROX)
X = CAMERA POSITIONS AND ALTERNATIVE POSITIONS
.......... = DAILY INSPECTION TRIP
–.–.–.– = LIMITS OF BAMBOO AND CEDAR FOREST.
..."WE ALWAYS HAD TO KEEP ROUGH CHARTS IN ORDER NOT TO LOSE THE CAMERAS...."

other, higher roof of cedars and other mighty trees. This double cover kept out much of the light but none of the rain.

Gander too, although he had great theories of always knowing where he was, was just as lost as I.

We kept on a few of the porters to work in camp and we got ourselves a Wanderobo in order not to spend our entire time being lost. Wanderobos are a kind of African Gypsy. They are of no separate tribe, but are merely odd members of various tribes who have taken to the forests, living vagrant lives illicitly trapping. Our Wanderobo was like a little tame gnome and he flitted about in and out of the forest with never a step in a false direction. He could lead you straight to a camera trap set seven or eight miles away from camp through a tangled world of meandering trails—and to him black cotton trip-wires stretched across dark corners might well have been six-inch wire hawsers painted white, for he never touched one.

If I ever found my way out to a camera site, I could never find my way back. My kind of signposts are good big sensible things with arrows and large lettering—one tiny nick with a panga as blaze-mark on just one of the hundreds of bamboo stems is no good at all to me. Tiny marks on the grassy trails, disturbed leaves, poky little indentations in the ground or blades of grass bent over, all proof that we had come this way on the way out, were quite invisible to me on the return journey. All ways looked alike, but to the little gnome it was as though we walked with whitewash on our boots.

We learned a lot from him about the interpretation of spoor. I found, both from him and later from the pygmies, that it was possible not only to tell what animals had gone along the game trails, but also more or less what size they were, how long ago they went this way, and practically what they were thinking about at the time. On muddy ground even I could see a legible imprint here and there, but I was hanged if I could spot anything on grassy paths. It made one feel very small to be so blind and to get so easily lost. I used to comfort myself occasionally by planning to take a Wanderobo to my own particular kind of jungle, to London, to see what he would make of that. . . . We did once take one into Nairobi. He was so scared that he would lose himself that he stayed all morning with one hand firmly clasping the door handle of the car . . . and after that I felt much better.

For the camp site we made a small clearing in the bamboos where there was a ledge in the hillside that fell away steeply down to the river Chania some four hundred feet below. The river Chania had its source somewhere back in the mountains and it wound its way mysteriously through exciting places. . . . It eventually finds its way, which is more than I could do, to Thika, and passes quite close to Nairobi. We came to know the Chania well. It was always cropping up in front of us, when, by all the laws of Gander's navigation it should have been behind us . . . and it was one of those rivers that look deceptively easy to cross by jumping from boulder to boulder. We crossed it this way many times and more often than not the boulders were just a little wider apart than we thought.

I don't know how I can adequately describe the feelings one has the first time one sleeps out without protection in a thick dark forest which is alive with wild animals both great and small. It is, I suppose, the thing that takes one to places like Africa, and which, in the end, sends one back again for more.

It is, somehow, the beginning . . . a going back, if you like, to the beginning . . . to the discovery that all the strange fears that one started with in the night-nursery are still only barely concealed beneath the false security of civilization. . . . It is a sudden realization of the inadequacy of man as man, stripped of all the accoutrements with which he has surrounded himself to bolster up his confidence. You are still a man—you haven't changed overnight—and yet you go back to being

A tiny island of light in a great black sea of bamboos. Camp at Night. (*Aberdares—10,000 ft.*)

a child. . . . The pitifully bright cloak of sophistication you have taken all these years to weave around your nakedness suddenly, and unfairly, falls away . . . and there you are . . . and you have to begin again . . . and the exciting part of it is that you suddenly begin to live intensely—just as a child does.

At night-time the forest, which has been quiet all day, suddenly comes to life and all around you there are noises and sounds which to you, as a babe in the woods, need explaining. . . . Camp, with its comforting fire, is like a tiny warm island in the middle of a great black sea, in which all manner of things are living, and moving—and watching. . . . You crawl into your sleeping bag and lie down, and gradually the fire dies, and you lie awake as the great black sea gradually washes up over your island and you.

We slept out many a night in many a dark forest. Inevitably one learns—the sounds all have their explanations—but the magic never goes. In the forests of the night there is always magic.

But here was an entirely different proposition from our lake-shore and the tunnels and the obliging hippopotamus. Here was a place of no horizon and no boundary, an endless tangle of jungle in which a myriad trails and paths went seemingly aimlessly in all directions. . . . This was a place of movement where the animals lived by the laws of the jungle and some were hunters and some were hunted—and in consequence their movements were not so easily predictable. Even twenty cameras in a place like this—however cunningly concealed and set — might have to wait a long time before rewards would come. Twenty cameras in fifty million bamboos can look very lost.

Those first few days we covered a lot of ground. We seldom came to the end of a day without having covered fifteen miles, and fifteen miles in the Aberdares is more like twenty-five in England's green and pleasant land. Panga in hand, slashing at the bamboos to make a path, topee on head, bearded chin and all, we began to look the part. We were rather impressed, and we were constantly taking photographs of ourselves (deliberately this time) in pioneering poses in order to be able to impress our friends, and possibly ourselves, later on.

We soon became aware of the large variety of game that lived and moved around us, and of the existence of the two plums we were after—the bongo and the giant forest hog. So far as I know, and I am the first to admit that my knowledge of these things is curiously limited, there *are* no adequate photographs of these two relatively recently discovered animals—leastways none taken of them at liberty in their own natural surroundings.

At this point I think it is time that I made myself plain, if I haven't done so already, that I am no zoologist, and that I am neither qualified, nor very willing, to enter into public correspondence with anyone signing himself "Game-warden for 20 years" or "Accuracy at all costs" in the columns of any paper. Gander would have loved it, and he would have done it very well—particularly in cases where he was obviously in the wrong.

By dint of searching we discovered a salt-lick that was evidently favoured by bongo, and also a place on the river where it seemed they watered fairly often. We also found a muddy spot where a giant forest hog took his mudbath. We found a lot of things . . . a cave where porcupine lived—a fallen tree which bushbuck jumped—a place where otter lived—and countless other places—and we made our plans and set our traps accordingly. It took us most of a week to set up seventeen cameras—and when it was done we found we had wandered so far afield that it was a long day's work to make a full inspection round all the sites.

We found a salt-lick on a small clear ledge among the bamboos. SETTING A CAMERA.

Bush Buck at Salt Lick. He came that night—and the result had much of the delicacy of a Japanese print.

Whether we made an abnormal amount of noise doing all this, or whether it was because a pack of wild dogs moved into the area, or whether there was some reason that was clear to the animals and obscure to us, I do not know, but for the first week the animals appeared to desert our area of the forest—and day after day we had no results at all. At length we decided to give the place a chance and we went off and climbed Mount Kinangop, leaving the cameras where they were. This took us two days and involved spending a night out in the open under a cliff some three hundred feet from the summit. For our pains we were rewarded with some unspectacular views of thick cloud banks seen from the inside. On the way down it started to rain, and for the next ten days it rained, on and off, more or less continuously—and we and our clothes, both on and off, were soaking wet for practically all that time.

We forgot our wetness in the discovery that, in our absence, things had started to happen with our camera traps. But with this change in fortune came a whole new series of snags that taxed our patience to the full.

When we got back we found that eleven out of the seventeen traps showed conclusive evidence that the animals had returned to their old haunts. On our rounds that day, moving about as quietly as we could, we saw a lot of game ourselves, including a family of giant forest hog—and yet, in the evening, returning home in the dark, we had an unpleasant time being followed and surrounded by wild dogs. But when we had closely examined each camera trap we found that all was not so rosy as we thought.

Condensation on the lenses was the worst trouble—and the rainy weather and the general steamy dampness hadn't helped at all. We later found that we had lost a lot of good pictures from blurred lenses, including one that would have been a beauty of two leopards together.

We slept out in the open under a cliff just below the summit. The scene at dawn had something of an early Italian painting. . . . Mt. Kinangop—(*12,500 ft.*)

A long, long trail awinding. PORTERS FOLLOWING AN ELEPHANT TRAIL.

But condensation wasn't all. It seemed that spiders could think of no nicer place to spin their webs than all across the front of a Leica camera. . . . It appeared that electric batteries, which I had never suspected of having any nourishing qualities at all, were considered most acceptable by ants—for they had swarmed into one synchroniser and they left the battery in there in very poor shape. . . . The birds too, particularly partridges, were apparently either more clumsy in these parts or else more malicious, for on several occasions they robbed us of pictures by carelessly flying or strolling through the black cotton trips. A misunderstanding also arose between us and the monkeys.

It was pure delight to see a troop of Colobus monkeys flying through the tree tops . . . lovely, lucky creatures with their long hair and feathery tails streaming out behind them . . . but they would insist, in our absence, on fooling about in the trees directly above our traps, and the general disturbance they created among the bamboos was very liable to snap the cotton trips. They either did that, or became curious about the cameras themselves and played around with these until the inevitable would occur.

And finally we also found that heavy rain by itself was liable to break the cotton and make the cameras take purely climatic pictures. . . . And so it went on—just one damn thing after another.

We began to live and think and talk and dream only in terms of cameras and animals, and the problems involved in getting the two of them to work together. Far from this becoming a boring one-track subject, the more we did and the more we learned the more engrossing and satisfying it became.

We stayed up in those forests, at somewhere in the neighborhood of ten to eleven thousand feet above sea-level, for the best part of three weeks—and towards the end it rained so much that everything in camp, including our bedding, was reduced to a soggy papier-mâché state, and it no longer made any difference to us whether we fell into the river or not. But somehow, even the constant rain didn't seem to matter, and, for myself, I have seldom felt so well as I did in the Aberdares.

Since leaving Africa, at the end of 1939, I have travelled a long way. I have found myself having to live out and move about in a number of mountain ranges, but even the problems of snow and extreme cold were simple compared with the rain and tangle of those bamboo forests. I know of only one place where movement was slower across country. That was in the crazy assault-courses of deadfall and fallen tree trunks that you find in burnt over sections of the forests in the back parts of British Columbia.

On the other hand I know of only one jungle, and it is not in Africa, where you cannot live unprotected on level terms with the animals—and that is in Whitehall. Elephant and leopard, snake and giant hog, these are as nothing compared with the denizens that lurk in the dark and twisting corridors of the War Office. For the innocent visitor to that deep jungle, however carefully he treads on his (and other) toes, there is little hope of survival. At any moment he may be mauled by major generals, snarled at by staff officers, or savaged by trumpeting brigadiers. . . . The Aberdares and the gorilla forests of the Congo are safer by far. . . .

Whilst we were on this second trial of our equipment in the Aberdares we had, from one reason or another, some forty actual "catches" with our trip-wires. But this time we knew better than to expect forty pictures . . . counting all the snags we had met, we finally agreed that we could reasonably expect a minimum of fifteen. We went back to Nairobi and had the films developed. We had five pictures. Twenty cameras, three weeks work, forty flash-bulbs—five pictures . . . that was how it went.

He came unexpectedly, to a place where we were awaiting a leopard. The trip wire ran across the trail from the bamboo stem in the top right hand corner of the picture. WHITE TAILED MONGOOSE.

We missed the giant forest hog. We got leopard, bushbuck, mongoose, and to our joy, the rare bongo.

To get what is probably the first picture of the bongo was no mean achievement. I was so elated that it took a great deal of dissuasion on Gander's part to prevent me festooning the hotel corridors with camera traps. I was sure, and I still am, that we would have secured some highly interesting results on nocturnal movements.

We actually got the bongo twice—the same animal. The first picture showed him about to cross the Chania river. The second picture showed only a portion of a very startled bongo having charged through the river and broken a trip-wire set on the far bank.

* * *

We got the rare Bongo.

Only a portion of a very startled Bongo.

# CHAPTER VI: BAD LANGUAGE

We had only been in Africa for a very little while before we became nicely involved in the language problem. The "Swahili" we were so proud of, and which we had studied so assiduously on our sooty voyage from Marseilles to Mombasa, had, up till now, served us reasonably well. We often found, however, that with the African we were largely left in the dark when lengthy answers repaid our questions. This, however, was no one-sided business . . . the African himself was often noticed to have difficulty in understanding his own language. We did, however, improve as we went along.

It was never very good Swahili that we spoke. We bothered hardly at all with grammar and, in common with the majority of Kenya settlers, we found that every sentence ended by being couched in the imperative and accompanied by sweeping and confident gestures. With strangers I was always a little uncertain of complete understanding, but with Njoki I was on firmer ground. He was my show piece. I could always be certain that when I gave him an order about something he would not stand foolishly around looking embarrassed. He would go off promptly and do something. It was not necessarily what I wanted him to do, but it was always something.

There was the occasion when I wanted some boot polish, and said so at some length—and Njoki came back proudly bearing a brand new household broom. There was also the time when a look of great tolerance came over his black face as, on my direct orders, he went out sadly into the hotel garden and hung my pyjamas on a string in the pouring rain. I left them there for two days just to show that occasionally we white men do put our pyjamas out in the pouring rain.

But the trouble was that even this mastery of the Swahili language was of comparatively little use to us in the Congo. What exactly were the languages the natives spoke in those parts was never very clear to us—but the strange thing was that conversation, instead of flagging, increased. This may possibly have been due to the sudden inclusion, as a kind of lowest of low common denominators to all concerned, of French. Any race of people that either speaks French, or has had French thrust upon it, always seems to speak it a very great deal.

I can speak French reasonably well, but am sensibly hesitant about it for fear of making ridiculous mistakes. Gander could speak it far less well, but suffered from no such inhibition. He, on the other hand, spoke far better Swahili than I—and yet I was often more voluble in this language than he. In this manner we sometimes found, when addressing a third party, that we were both talking about two entirely different subjects. In East Africa this often resulted in getting things done a great deal quicker. In the Belgian Congo, when French came into play, we found we had to modify our approach.

The result was that our utterances quickly became a brilliantly cunning concoction of Swahili, English, French, together with a wealth of gesture and a word or two of German

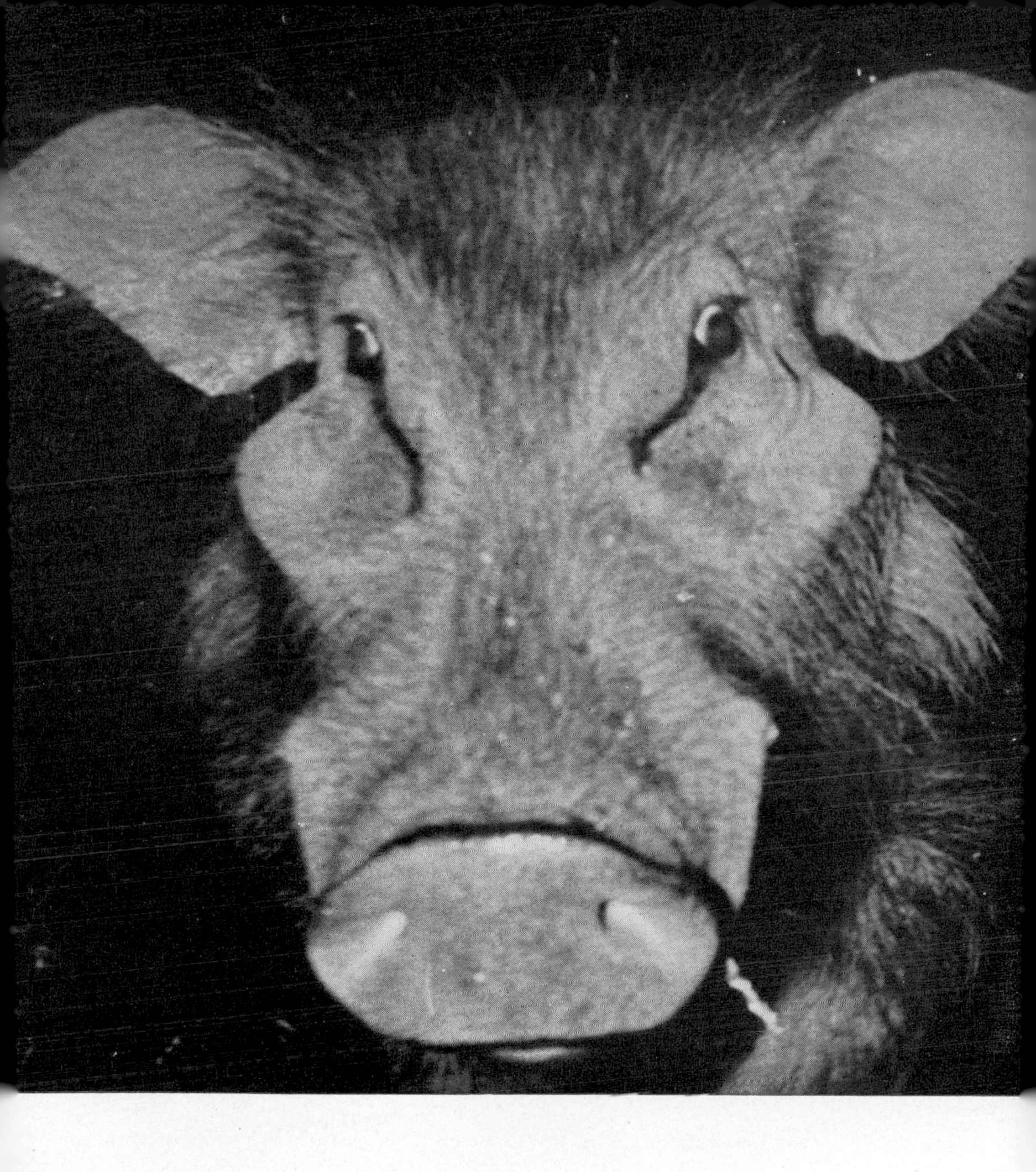

Bad language? GIANT FOREST HOG.

We often used bad language when this kind of thing happened. . . . DIK DIK.

to make the thing clear, so that there could be no possible room for misunderstanding. The only difficulty was that it was very seldom we met with either native or Belgian official sufficiently gifted to reply with similar ease and clarity. This was a very great pity and generally seemed to involve our audiences in widespread and tiresome search for anyone who had a few words of English at his command.

Time, however, is of little consequence in Africa, and, taking an overall picture of the many and complicated conversations we had with a wide variety of obstinately uni-lingual peoples and tribes, we came to the conclusion that it was merely a matter of dogged perseverance for the white man, with his superior intellectual equipment, to win through. For anyone who, during this war, has witnessed the British Tommy or the American G.I. making himself abundantly clear to the inhabitants of strange and dark lands, this point is now adequately proven.

I feel, however, that I do not have to stress the point that it was not always easy. For two parties devoid of a common language it is a relatively simple matter for the one to bring home to the other the fact that he is hungry, or thirsty, or merely lost, or, provided the facial muscles are elastic, that he wants to see a gorilla. In the same situation it is by no means so easy to explain the necessity for taking twenty small black boxes out into the deepest forest and hiding them in certain strategic thickets and for festooning the elephant trails with electric light bulbs and yards of black cotton. . . . We had, of course, a wide range of gestures that accompanied each performance, but even these were not always perfectly understood. The pygmies were particularly obtuse.

I deplore the use of heavy sarcasm, but, in moments of frustration, I sometimes found myself wondering what on earth would have become of the primitive tribes of Central

Africa had not the white man come along with his culture, and inventive genius—and tireless perseverance.

At one point we were very kindly offered the chance of employing one man as interpreter who, it was claimed, spoke fluent English. From what stock he sprang was never clear, for he appeared to combine a little of every stock, and his opening remarks led one to suspect that there was a monkey or two swinging about somewhere in his family tree.

"How long have you lived here?" asked Gander.

"I was here for seven days next week—and after that I was for six years in Irumu . . . "

We smiled approvingly and after we had had a little more in like vein we decided that we preferred our own brand of Esperanto and the direct approach.

It is perhaps worth mentioning at this juncture the slight technical embarrassment that confronts a traveler when he is writing or speaking of animals. Does he refer to a particular animal in the singular or the plural? Does one, in other words, go to the Congo after gorilla? or after gorillas? With most big game animals there is, as far as the literary side is concerned, no embarrassment. For some reason, it is fairly generally accepted that one goes after lion, or tiger, or rhino—and you somehow cannot go out on safari after elephants in the plural. It all has to be, and is, singular. Yet on the other hand, you most certainly do not visit zoos to offer peanuts to elephant. So where are you? There may well be only one elephant in the zoo to accept your peanuts, yet he must be in the plural. Equally you may find yourself surrounded by scores of elephants in Congo forests and yet they have to be in the singular—and in this case it is more correct, and certainly more impressive to say, "I went out after elephant."

But does one go after gorilla? or after gorillas? It is a nice point. I, personally, like to think of the gorilla as something very exceptional in the way of animals and so, in order to make him a little different from other forms of big game, I have decided to take a firm line and address him in the plural.

* * *

The Hyrax is reputed to be the Biblical Coney. At night-time in the forest he is responsible for very startling noises.

Curiously enough his three toed feet prove him to be a relative of the Rhino. HYRAX

# CHAPTER VII: THE EQUATOR

The drive across to the Congo from Nairobi was brim full of interest. With the many last minute things we found we had to do in Nairobi, and taking into consideration the absurdly high proportion of extremely attractive girls who did so like to be taken out dancing in the evening, we eventually got away, more or less true to form, only a week behind the schedule we had set for ourselves.

We found that the driver's cabin of the lorry was a great deal more comfortable and dustproof to ride in than the station wagon Ford, so Gander and I went ahead in the truck, followed by Njoki and Jepharia in the "B'wana's" car, riding in style and looking and acting as though the whole expedition was their affair and their organization. Deceptive, I admit —but only up to a point.

I have been to many lands since those days and have travelled many thousands of miles, dressed rather unconvincingly as a soldier, but none so far has held the attention so faithfully, minute by minute almost, as did Africa. It is true, for my part anyway, that it is greatly difficult to travel

CAMOUFLAGE. Unless you know where to look the Hyrax is difficult to spot.

about Central Africa and not be interested all the time. There always seems to be something new to see, or to hear, or to search for . . . I suppose I have an advantage. I have what I might perhaps call a penchant for animals. I don't know very much about them, but I just like them. I even draw animals in an indifferent and unflattering kind of way, and insist on publishing these drawings as children's books—which the public, rightly, very largely ignores.

When you drive, as we did, across a very large slice of Central Africa you can see any number of different kinds of animals. Even only a mile or two outside Nairobi you are liable to run into—literally, if you are not careful—large herds of zebra and wildebeeste and other animals of the plains, and as like as not you may be lucky enough to see lion. Ostrich, baboon, bush pig, giraffe, and so on . . . they are all there . . . maybe not on the main road, but not far off . . . and you can often take quite impressive photographs without even getting out of the car. At night time it is sometimes even more spectacular—when you round a bend and there, suddenly, standing majestically in the glare of the headlights is something that you know perfectly well ought to be safely inside some Zoo. The first time I saw elephants at large, down at Namanga that was, it took me a little while to realize that it wasn't possible to stroll up and ingratiate oneself with peanuts. This feeling is far more pronounced when you are safely seated in a car than when prowling about on your own in a forest.

I am well aware that I am laying myself wide open to the sternest criticism for taking ingenuousness just one step too far by making remarks like that—but it is a fact. I often found I had to pinch myself quite hard to realise that here were no bars or cages or enclosures—and that any amount of peanuts was no passport to popularity.

The journey across was slow, as we were forever stopping the cars to inspect this or that and to take photographs. I had

Sometimes one can take quite good photographs without even getting out of the car.

Difficult subjects to photograph. Locusts.

never seen a swarm of locusts before—far less driven a car like a juggernaut through one. I had never seen a lake pink with countless thousands of flamingoes, or a road black with countless millions of hoppers, or a golf course where there was a local rule about picking out of hippo footprints without penalty, or the source of the Nile, or people walking about in the open in their birthday suits happily indifferent to clothing coupons, or a countryside which at one point appeared to be largely on fire, or such bad roads, or a thousand and one other things. The trees were new trees to me, so were the butterflies, and the villages and the crops . . . and practically everything that you cared to look at.

It would be a pleasure to inflict the reader with minute descriptions of all these things, and with one's reactions to all this "newness," but I will be reasonable—better men by far than I have done it all before, and the reader can easily be spared much of the wind that fills these sails.

We took six days on that journey—driving more or less along the equator from east to west until we had crossed Kenya and Uganda and come to the frontier of the Belgian Congo. We stayed in hotels and roadhouses on the way, which, although they are few and far between, were all of them marvelously comfortable and whose hosts were invariably hospitable to a degree. It was not that these places were always without eccentricities—it is one of the delights of Kenya and Uganda that you constantly come across people who allow full rein to any slight eccentricities they may have.

There was one man who ran a hotel, miles from anywhere, who would accept you with every grace as a guest as long as you pulled up your car *behind* his hotel. If you pulled up in front of his place, wild horses wouldn't make him take you in. We were merely fortunate in choosing the back.

There was, further on, a delightful lady who ran a very fine and efficient hotel in spite of a reed-buck called Mark, a monkey that used a mirror and really chewed tobacco, two cranes that flew up and danced for their dinner, two dachshunds, various cats, one tame and two disrespectful parrots, and, somewhere or other, a husband.

We finally came to the frontier at Kisoro where, in spite of our curious and dutiable cargo of equipment, we had an easy passage owing to a previous hard day's work on the customs officials at Kampala. There followed the short no-man's land and then the Belgian frontier. Here we had an equally easy passage due to letters of introduction from Brussels—for which I had to thank my very good friend, Johnny Wittouck.

And so, eventually, we came to the strange new scenery of the Belgian Congo.

* * *

THE MOUNTAIN FORESTS

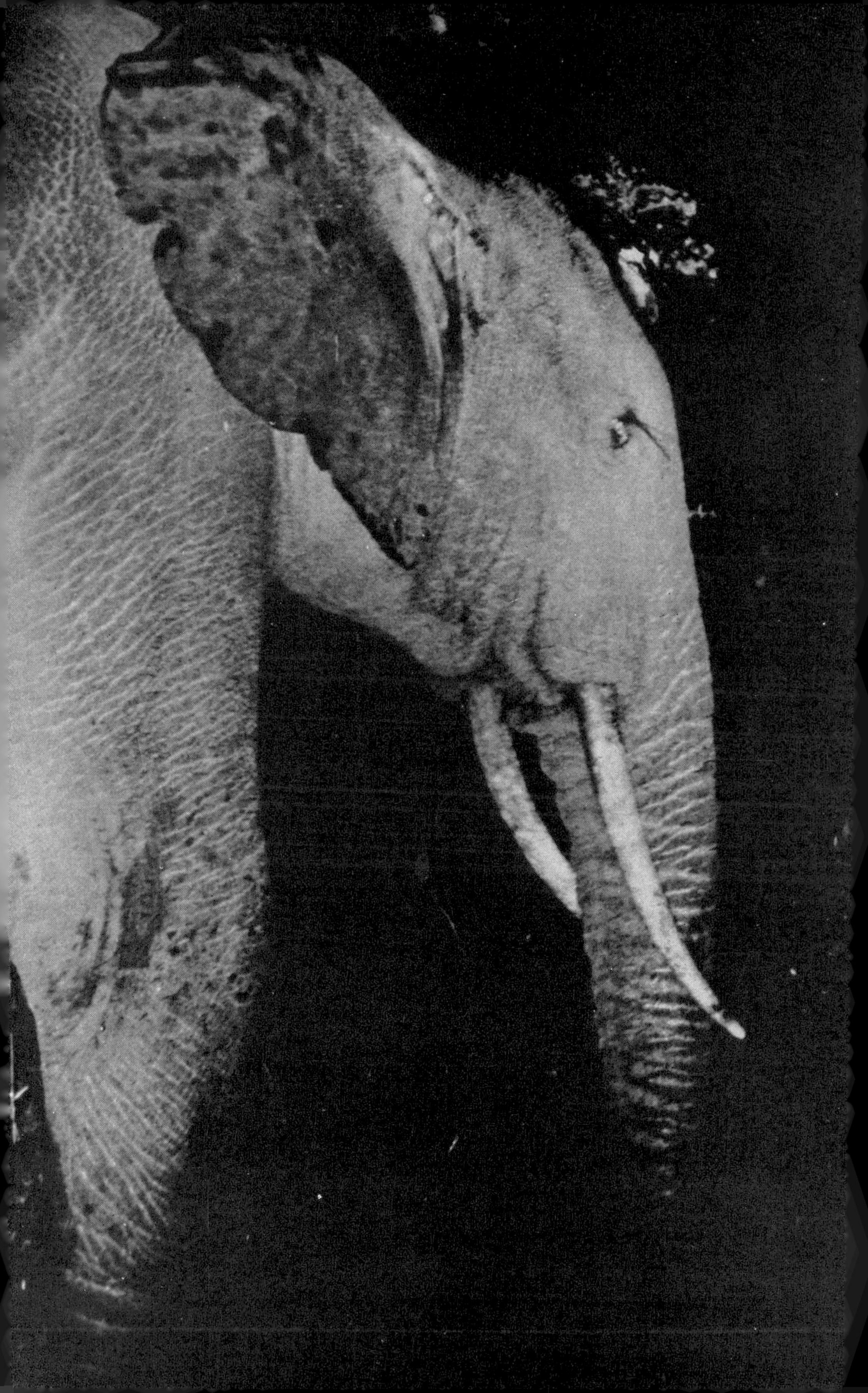

# CHAPTER VIII: VOLCANOES

Our introduction to the Congo was scarcely encouraging. We arrived at the little hotel on the lakeshore of Kivu on the same evening as a party from the University at Johannesburg, but these people, students and professors, had met with a serious accident that day. A few miles back from the lake the road runs through a section of the forest at the foot of Mount Mikeno in which elephant can always be found. We came to know it well ourselves later on when we moved in there and camped in the middle of it, and often found ourselves living in close company with as many as two hundred elephants. But as we listened to the story this party had to tell that evening we began to look at one another sideways.

It seems that the car in which the party was travelling was a large eight-seater of American make. They had spotted some elephant quite close to the road and had stopped the car, and, which was a mistake, the engine as well—and were busy taking photographs. It was during this that one of the elephants took exception to their presence and charged the car. For some reason the engine refused to start up again. The occupants

In the forests at the foot of Mount Mikeno.

tumbled out as fast as they could to run for cover—all save one. He was half out of the car when the elephant hit it. Its tusks went through the side panels and up through the roof, and it turned the big car right over on top of the last man who was half out of the far door. The elephant then proceeded to shove the overturned car around much as though it was an objectionable petrol can being kicked around by a small boy.

It appears that eventually the elephant burnt its trunk on the hot exhaust manifold, for it dashed away suddenly and then, curiously enough, fell over and died. And there were the two corpses, one large car and one large elephant, separated only by some fifty yards. But underneath the former was a badly crushed professor with broken legs and a smashed pelvis.

They got him out alive and brought him in to Goma—and did the best they could for him. We arrived just in time to help get him into the building. They made a makeshift stretcher out of a wooden door and pillows and all that night in the hotel the poor man screamed in agony as there was no morphia or other means to quell his pains. During the night two others of the party drove four hundred miles to Kampala to bring rescue.

The next evening, miraculously it seemed, a plane arrived from Nairobi and made a precarious landing, and the injured man was flown to hospital. We heard later that he subsequently recovered.

It was a sobering night, that first night at Goma.

It is difficult to describe the country in which we suddenly found ourselves. Before leaving England, I had read a number of books on this part of the world, including Carl Akeley, Martin Johnson and Attilio Gatti. I must perhaps have overdone the scepticism with which the town-dweller is apt to treat most travel books, and particularly those that deal with "My Encounters With Big Game," for I still retained my school-boy conception of what Equatorial Africa, and certainly the very center of it, ought to look like. Before I went there I never properly realised that there were any mountains worth considering as mountains, let along volcanic mountains, in the middle of the dark continent—but I received a very considerable shock when I did eventually get there myself. Even after having seen Stromboli and Vesuvius and Etna on the way out, and compared their activities unfavourably with those of the sinister funnel of our ship, and even after having lived for some years on the edge of every kind of political volcano in England, I was still not prepared for the sight that greets one as one climbs to the top of the Kinaber Pass and looks for the first time into the Congo.

There, spread out before one, is an impossibly dramatic panorama of a beautiful but utterly fantastic world.

I find myself no longer a very attentive listener when someone is extolling the beauties of Scotland or the South Downs—and claims that there is nothing finer in the world. True, there is nothing in the world quite the same as Scotland or the South Downs. England is always England, and, God help us, always will be. . . . But I should dearly love to own a private magic carpet on which to whisk the faithful and untravelled patriot to scenes of wider scope—to a balcony in the Alpina Hotel in Mürren—to Wadi Rum in Arabia—to the Kinaber Pass in the Congo—to the Bella Coola Valley in British Columbia . . . quickly—just like that. . . . And, when we got back, I would be happy and interested to discuss Scotland and the South Downs until very early on in the morning . . .

But right now I am in the Congo. The scenery suddenly seems to consist largely of volcanoes—and "largely" is the only possible word, for the major peaks are somewhere just short of fifteen thousand feet—while the many minor ones have to be content with a paltry ten thousand or so.

I don't know exactly how many of these volcanoes there are in sight at one glance—but there are at least nine out-

NYNAGONGA AND NYAMLAGIRA. Looking across native cultivation (shambas) in the foreground to two active volcanoes.

standingly large ones. Some of these have had their day and are extinct; others are grumbling and anxious to assert themselves; and one or two are busy being very active indeed. It was all rather disturbingly symbolical of the Europe of 1937-38 that we had just left.

Apart from the winding road, which is of fairly recent construction, a few native villages, and here and there a blinding example of the white man's constructional ability, there is little else save forest and wild country. Set in the middle of this is the beautiful blue Lake Kivu.

The reader may or may not remember a few years ago seeing a modest little paragraph in the newspapers which announced, for those that were interested, that a volcano in Central Africa had erupted with some violence. It doesn't matter—when it was pointed out to me by Gander at the time, I was far more interested in the social entries scrawled in my own diary—and only gave it the same fleeting attention that the Londoner used to give to the major disaster that occurred happily so far, far away. When, some two years later, I saw this volcano myself, it was a very different story.

Nyamlagira, for that is this particular mountain's name, is by no means one of the bigger or more ferocious volcanoes—on the contrary, it is comparatively unassuming and retiring—yet it has been erupting fairly solidly ever since the day when it exploded, and, in its own quiet way, has done just as well, if not better, than Vesuvius did, even when the latter was at the top of its form. What is more, Nyamlagira did the same thing in 1912—and will probably do it again—on the apparent basis of a violent eruption a couple of years before all European wars. It stands, this mountain, some fifteen to twenty miles back from the northern coast of Lake Kivu, but now it is connected to the lake by a stream of lava of its own making, some four to five miles wide. The little road that rounded one section of the edge of the lake now disappears under this vast stream and is blocked and lost, together with countless square miles of forest and bush.

When we saw it, this lava, still red hot, was constantly pouring into the lake and the clouds of steam that resulted could be seen from miles away. We clambered cautiously over the four to five mile width of this stream on the more or less solid upper crust of the lava until we came to the small native village of Sake, which miraculously escaped destruction and which is now completely cut off from Goma. There we got hold of a native canoe—an unconvincing craft that was simply a hollowed-out tree trunk—which balanced right way up in the water by faith alone, and paddled ourselves gingerly over to where the lava stream flowed into the lake. The sight and sound were worthy of one of Hollywood's more expensive disasters. It was impossible to go closer than about one hundred yards, and even at that distance the lake water became so hot that it began to affect our canoe, and we had to return. They told us in Sake that when the lava first came rushing into the lake a great quantity of fish came rushing up to the surface, cooked and ready to serve . . . a "Munchausen" that I can readily believe.

The game warden of this area, a gentleman of some importance by the name of Colonel Hoier, who was later to become not only an enthusiastic helper to our cause, but also a very good friend, had the extraordinary experience of being actually down in the crater of Nyamlagira taking records when the mountain blew up. He lived to tell the tale because the eruption was of such intensity that it blew a hole right through the side of the mountain way down near the level of the plain, instead of taking the more normal and easier course, upwards, via Colonel Hoier.

Next to Nyamlagira stands Ninagonga.

They have attractive names these volcanoes . . . Nyamlagira, Ninagonga, Visoke, Mikeno, Karasimbi . . . and there is even

NYNAGONGA VOLCANO SEEN FROM MOUNT MIKENO. The rest of Africa seemed an awful long way down below.

a cheeky little one called Hehu, which is inhabited by chimpanzees. Ninagonga, too, is in constantly angry mood. By day a great plume of smoke comes from the cone, and by night the sky reflects the glow from the fires raging in the crater. A constant check is kept on the level of the lava, inside the crater, which rises and falls many feet in accordance with Ninagonga's temper. It is, I suppose, only a matter of time before this volcano imitates her neighbour—and, when that happens, the people of the little native villages of Goma and Kiseni on the edge of the lake will have to do some pretty quick thinking. . . . And whether they think quickly enough or not there will be just another modest little paragraph in "The Times."

The two volcanoes Mikeno and Karasimbi are extinct—but they are the two highest and in many ways are more impressive than their adolescently bumptious neighbours. These two mighty mountains are joined together by a saddle at between the ten and eleven thousand feet level at a place which is known as Kabara. When you stand up there on that broad ridge at Kabara, Mikeno towers over you on the one hand with its peak at fourteen thousand seven hundred, and Karasimbi on the other rises to the fifteen thousand foot mark.

Kabara is a place of animals, and, dominating all the animals that live and move in the tangled forest around Kabara, are gorillas. It was here at Kabara that Martin Johnson camped for most of his search after gorillas. It is a wonderful, mysterious place—a beautiful fairy land, inhabited by almost everything but fairies. Martin Johnson apparently never ventured up Mount Mikeno. He called it "The Mountain Without a Top"—and that is nearly always apt, because Mikeno generally hides its head in angry clouds.

It is at Kabara that the most famous of the gorilla hunters, Carl Akeley, is buried. His grave is marked by a simple carved stone, surrounded by a split log fence. He loved this place

Kabara Camp. 10,500 Feet. A lovely place on the saddle between Mikeno and Karasimbi.

with a true love, as you have only to read his wife's book to discover, and he is probably content to lie in the midst of his "... most beautiful spot in all the world ..." He was the man who was largely responsible for persuading the Belgian authorities to protect the gorillas and he provided much information about the boundaries required for establishing the great National Albert Park as a wild and undisturbed sanctuary. (It is a pity that the word "Park" had to be used, for Mikeno and the surrounding country is anything but a park). He has another memorial to his name that will live for a very long time. This is the series of groups that have been constructed in the Akeley Memorial Hall of African Mammals in the American Museum of Natural History in New York City. These beautiful and faithfully accurate groups have been constructed from the specimens and paintings that Akeley and his staff collected in the Congo, and they are more than well worth a visit.

Karasimbi is simply a vast great cone going straight up to an impressive fifteen thousand feet. When I first saw it the top thousand feet of the cone was covered in snow—and, more often than not, the mountain wears a neat little ring of cloud around its peak, like a white fur collar—just to make everything symmetrical.

Mount Mikeno is not like the other volcanoes. To get to the top of all the rest simply involves struggling uphill through very dense forests (until you reach the tree line) for a very long time—say two days up and two days down—but Mikeno is different. You still have to do the struggling uphill, considerably steeper struggling, for a couple of days, but when you have finished that you find that the mountain has collected itself and thrown itself up into a final thousand feet of rock face before it is satisfied with its peak. From the plains down below, Mikeno has a fierce inaccessible look about it, which is intensified by its habit of only occasionally allowing you

Mount Karasimbi. A pure cone rising to 15,000 feet.

alarming little peeps at its topmost crags and pinnacles—for, as I have said, it is almost continuously hidden in angry-looking clouds.

When we were camped down at its foot trying for pictures of elephant I used to regard this fact as a great blessing, because we had already decided we were going to try to climb Mikeno, and every time I caught glimpses of the final summit it used to do horrible things to my stomach.

* * *

MOUNT MIKENO. Different from the other volcanoes.

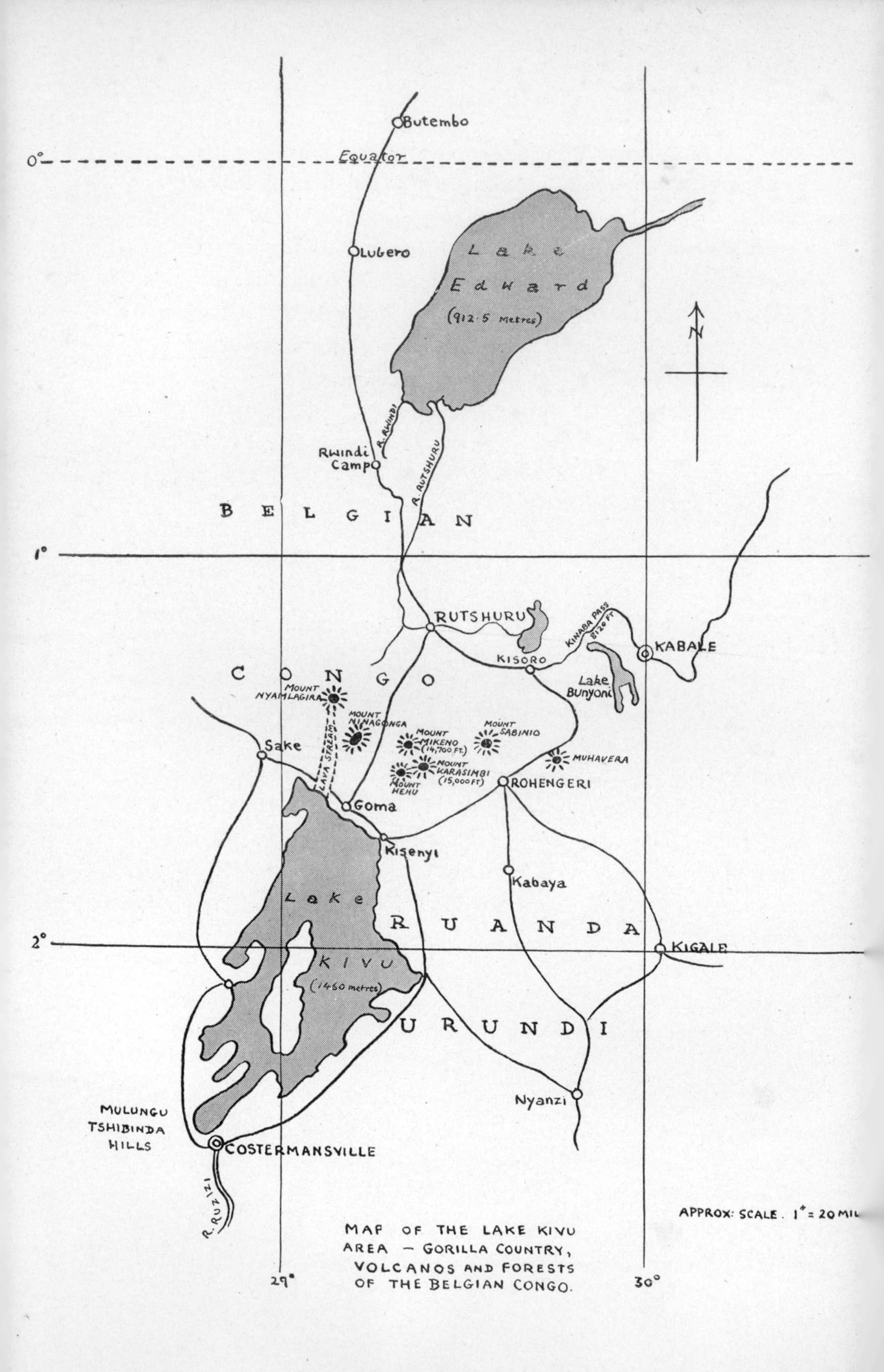


MAP OF THE LAKE KIVU AREA — GORILLA COUNTRY, VOLCANOS AND FORESTS OF THE BELGIAN CONGO.

# CHAPTER IX: THE RED CARPET

It was at about this time that I began to talk in my sleep. It was apparently mostly about animals. With one's entire waking hours spent in looking for, thinking about, and talking about animals, I claim that it is not unreasonable that they should begin to invade one's dreams. Gander used to tell me in the mornings what I had met overnight. My first encounter was with a lion—very close it was—right there at the foot of the camp bed to be exact—and Gander followed my running commentary with interest. If I may be permitted to use an ungrammatical zeugma, I appear, under the circumstances and the bedclothes, to have been quite reasonably brave.

The business of the moment, however, was to find out how best to encounter a gorilla in one's waking hours—with none of this nonsense at night.

We had at first to drive around in the car for considerable distances to meet the game wardens to whom we had letters of introduction from Professor Van Straelen of the Natural History Museum in Brussels. The National Albert Park is not a place into which anyone may wander at will and get on with whatever business he has in mind. Without very special permission, you may not even leave the few roads that pass through the area, or at best, the cross country tracks that are used in the lower lying regions of the Reserve for driving the keen (but not too keen) visitor around, so that he may return able to boast that he has seen a large selection of big game.

We were most anxious not to be restricted to roads and tracks and, in order to obtain our permits, we had had to satisfy Brussels that our photographic methods would not be likely to lead to trouble, and that we would do nothing whatsoever to harm or disturb the animals.

There was a time when the gorilla was in great danger of being exterminated. Prior to its protection hunters used to come from far and wide to shoot this greatest prize of them all. But now they have bred to sufficient extent to warrant survival, and it is only the scientifically minded or the innocently curious, who go out to look for them and study them, who are in any likelihood of extermination. Estimates have been made by various experts as to the exact numbers of gorillas alive in Central Africa—and they vary largely. One will say three hundred, another two thousand. In any case there is now no danger of the gorilla becoming extinct—unless it so happens that one section of the gorilla tribe turns totalitarian and the apes repay Hitler with the sincerest form of flattery. An exact estimate of their numbers is, I think, impossible, for they live in very inaccessible and thick country and are relatively seldom seen by anyone save the natives who live and have their shambas* in the neighbourhood of the Reserves.

There are three of these gorilla areas in the mountains of the Eastern Congo. One is the area around Luberu, north of Lake Kivu; another in the Tchibinda Hills south west of the lake; and the third, and probably the most important, on

* *Gardens, or cultivated areas.*

Mount Mikeno. I say this third one is the most important because it is the most strictly reserved and certainly the most interesting. No one is allowed on Mount Mikeno at all without the most complicated series of permits and papers. In none of these three Reserves is one allowed to carry a rifle, and this was all part of our contract with the authorities in Brussels, for to kill, or be killed by a gorilla are crimes without parallel to the Belgian Government. The penalties are very severe, and in one case, of course, automatic. To be killed by a gorilla, the verdict is that it was your own fault for being there—and that you went there fully aware that gorillas are apt to resent the presence of anything masquerading, however well, as one of them.

There were moments when I thought our contract a little one-sided and when I should have been happier had a representative gorilla been a co-signatory to the same agreement.

The two main officials to whom we had to present ourselves were Colonel Hoier, who lived at Romangabo, and Commandant Hubert, his second-in-command, who was based at Ruindi Camp. We went to them, armed with our impressive letters from Brussels, and we expected the red carpet to be laid for us. The reaction we got, however, was one of surprise welcome and very friendly hospitality, but so far as any permits were concerned they knew nothing at all about us whatsoever and, quite frankly, there was nothing doing. . . . In other words, no letter had come to them from Brussels and, whereas they regretted *infiniment,* there was absolutely *rien à faire*.

There followed a few days of confusion and cables and misunderstandings, during which we did our best to convince these two that all was really in order, and that something very African must have happened to Van Straelen's letter. Colonel Hoier, I am sure, was happy about our integrity and would, I think, have allowed us to continue with our plans, letter or no letter—but not so *le brave* Commandant Hubert. His was a volatile and flamboyant character and he was proud and jealous of his domain, and, with no letter, he would certainly not allow us anywhere on our own.

Hubert was renowned throughout the area for his temerity with the animals. He had the reputation for stopping the charging lion with a word of command and the power of the human eye and all that . . . I must say Hubert had quite an eye . . . and he took great delight in showing us endless rather blurred photographs, almost every second one of which showed some animal or other charging Hubert—yet here was *le brave* Commandant showing them to us himself, so something must have happened. . . . He was an interesting character and he knew his animals well. After he had taken us on a Cook's tour of the place I began to suspect that the reverse was also true and that some of the animals also knew Hubert very well indeed. . . . There was one lion that . . . well, never mind.

That Cook's tour was one of the least fortunate experiences we had in Africa and was typical of what can happen to a beautiful place the moment that its guardian becomes infected with the disease and desire to impress the visitor.

We were taken by Hubert in our own car, which he insisted on driving himself as we would certainly have proved unsafe, and we were told that on no account were we to get out of the car at any time. We began to suspect a "build-up." The ensuing ride proved infinitely more dangerous than a session with a rogue elephant ever could have been. With the car making a din like an oncoming express, we were plunged and bumped and whirled across country, at far too many miles an hour for safety or the springs, through, over, and under marsh, tussock, bush, and plain. . . . Three times we went into uncontrolled broadside skids and all but turned over, and once Gander was thrown clean out of the car. The Ford, everything and everybody, was covered from top to bottom with mud and we were both scared stiff by the vehicle which, for our own safety, we were not allowed to leave! We would gladly have walked home on foot. We advanced on various animals at a rate of knots, in what I imagine was supposed to be spectacular fashion—and the animals, very wisely, declined to hang around.

It was an incredibly stupid and unscientific performance, which was a very great pity, because the opportunities for photography (without a car) were on every hand. We saw buffalo, lion, hippo, elephant, and many other animals, and, had we been allowed two or three days to approach the various problems with a little thought and care, we could have had some wonderful results.

We returned from that Cook's tour depressed and unimpressed with *le brave* Commandant's methods. I like to think that perhaps he was having one of his off days.

A couple of days after this the situation became easier as the long-lost letter from Brussels was found to have arrived two months previously and to have remained unnoticed by anyone concerned—and at last the red carpet was ours. . . . From now on we had permission to leave the car and go wherever we wished. . . .

Colonel Hoier was a very different personality. He had none of the dash and flamboyance of Hubert and was, if anything, inclined to be shy and retiring, but he was extremely efficient and knowledgeable about the flora and fauna of the Congo and went a long way out of his way to be helpful and encouraging to us and our schemes. Whereas with Hubert we could not help feeling, however little it was intended, that our efforts were really rather laughable and that our freedom of movement was slightly resented, to visit Colonel Hoier in his little wooden house at Romangabo, or to have him come and stay with us in camp, was a very real pleasure.

On the Ruindi Plains. BUFFALO

Colonel Hoier advised us to go to Luberu for gorilla. He told us the natives in that area were more intelligent and helpful than in the Tchibinda Hills. Professor van Straelen in Brussels had advised us to go to the latter as the gorillas had been completely undisturbed in that area, whereas at Luberu they had been illegally shot up on one or two occasions and were consequently wilder. We put this to Hoier but he was of the opinion that there were so many gorillas at Luberu that it didn't matter very much and that with our system it was unlikely we would get into trouble. We ourselves wanted to go to Mount Mikeno, because there were many other animals there besides gorillas. So, in the end we decided to make a round trip and go to all three places . . . and in between these visits we planned to get going with the cameras on various lesser animals.

* * *

# CHAPTER X: NIGHT TIME

I realise now that it is the responsibility of the author of a travel book about Big Game to provide the reader with breath-taking descriptions of appalling danger. All the best-selling books on Africa have these on every other page and it is a constant surprise to the reader that the author has somehow maintained life and limb. When I was in Africa I never thought of things in quite this light. I'm afraid I was wholly engaged, much as I am in Piccadilly or Broadway, with the thought of how best to avoid unfortunate clashes with things bigger than myself. In the interest of royalties I ought really to have been eaten by a lion or something.

My safety precautions appear, from my diary, to have been less successful at night, so, in order to make this book more exciting, I must be permitted every now and again to recount my dreams. It seems that one night I sat up in my sleeping bag and suddenly woke Gander with the following definite statement.

"It's a tiger! My God—it's a tiger!"

To which Gander, who was awake, replied quite reasonably

We finally got permission to go into the fantastic forests.
PORTERS

that it couldn't be because there weren't any tigers in Africa. Burn they never so bright, in these forests of the night it *couldn't* be a tiger. . . .

But it *was* a tiger—and this reply brought forth the rather sheepish answer from me.

"I know . . . I'm awake . . . it's all right . . . I can see it's on a string. . . ."

Excitement, of course, was not limited to dreams for there were plenty of times when Africa provided quite adequate thrills for both of us. As things are, with nothing hair-raising to describe, I think the best thing I can do is to take the reader up a tree, and, if I am at all successful, perhaps to convey to him something of the beauty and mystery and magic of an African night.

First we need a tree—just one tree out of the many millions in the forests. Then we need a large full moon because we need to be able to see what is going on around us. Thirdly we need animals. . . . All these things are fortunately very easy to find. And lastly we have to forget what we have just been doing, and what we are just going to do, and live only in terms of the present. Apart from this generally being a good thing in any case, it is a very easy thing to do in the forests, for the present is far too fascinating to miss.

If one is going to be out all night, and if, as in this instance, a spot where there are a great number of elephants at large has been chosen, the first thing—as always—is to consider the safety angle.

We had been working in this particular area for about a fortnight and we had had a comparatively large number of successes with our cameras. We decided that we wanted to stay out a whole night through because it was obvious that a great deal of activity was suddenly taking place. The whole aspect of our camera area had suddenly changed overnight and hundred of trees and bushes had been pulled down and wrecked. Many new paths had been made everywhere, showing masses of fresh elephant spoor and droppings. Fortunately this time no cameras had been knocked down, although several of the trip-wire stakes themselves were snapped and broken, and, in one sector, seven out of eight cameras set about two miles away from camp had taken pictures overnight.

It took a full day's work to repair the damage and to reset the cameras and to find and prepare a suitable place in a suitable tree where we could spend the next night. We had to work quickly and quietly because we were conscious of considerable movement going on not far away from us—and on one occasion we had to run very fast.

We were lucky in finding an ideal tree right in the center of our camera trap area. Some six feet off the ground the tree branched up into three separate trunks which made it comparatively easy to wedge a sort of rough platform in between these trunks at a height of about twenty feet above ground. One must build at least as high as that because an elephant, with its very considerable height, using its trunk over and above that—and possibly also its forelegs on the trunk of the tree—can reach up a very long way. You have to take all this into consideration because if you happen to provoke an African elephant—and they are very liable to take exception to the most unreasonable things—events begin to happen very quickly. For example your mere scent, fortunately, so unnoticeable to those near and dear to you (save in the tabloid press advertisements), comes across to the sensitive elephant like a dose of mustard gas. When this happens he is just as likely as not to decide to wipe you off the face of the earth without further delay. You never can tell with elephants and they are, without any doubt, high up on the list of dangerous animals. Once an elephant has made this decision, since men cannot run as fast as he can, the only hope is to get as fast as possible as high as possible up the strongest tree you can find—and twenty feet

up is about the minimum. There are plenty of people alive to-day who had every reason to suspect that their tree climbing days were over long ago—but it only takes an angry elephant to bring out the Tarzan in one, even in the elderly tourist.

We climbed up on to our platform about an hour before sundown and pulled the rope up after us. Our boys left us to go back to camp—barely concealing their broad grins at the spectacle of two madmen looking slightly ridiculous half way up a tree on a ledge that was obviously far too small for them. Njoki was convinced that we had finally taken complete leave of our senses and I rather suspect his solicitude for our safety was due to the fact that he was wondering how on earth he was going to get all the way home to Nairobi all by himself.

Our tree stood right at the edge of a large elephant track which led down to a muddy water hole. Other tracks crossed and recrossed all around. There were about fifteen other large trees around us, well spaced out with nothing to impede visibility. Down below the undergrowth was high in places, but comparatively thin and we could see nearly all the tracks. It took some little time to settle in and arrange ourselves in the very small space, and, after a lot of shuffling around and whispered argument as to which bit of space belonged to which, we eventually got ourselves as comfortable as we could—and after that we stayed completely still.

It wasn't very long before we forgot all about comfort. . . .

If there had been any wind previously it too became still and not a leaf moved in the forest—and we were alone in the middle of a strange and lovely world of beauty and silence . . . a world which gave one a tingle all down the spine.

Presently things began to happen.

First there came the sounds of branches snapping and the crack of a tree breaking—some distance off—a pause, and then trumpeting. . . . Silence again, and tension—suddenly more

Up a Tree. One has to build fairly high. . . .

trumpeting, closer this time, and more crashing—and then nothing for quite a while.

If we had not both been watching the right spot we would never have seen the first elephant appear. The silence with which that great bulk approached was uncanny—and terribly impressive. He stole unconcernedly out of some bushes about eighty yards away, crossed right in front of us without making a sound, and walked silently into the shadows of another clump of bushes. It was as strange as looking at an old silent film.

Then, quite suddenly it seemed, with at least half an hour of daylight to go, there were elephants all around us. The show was on—and we had come the right night. From out of a tangle of undergrowth a few yards from us there suddenly appeared the eerie spectacle of a black sinuous trunk, waving vaguely in the air—and then the leaves and creepers parted and everything went prehistoric with the appearance of a pair of enormous tusks and a great head and monstrous flapping ears. And there was an elephant—close enough to hear him breathing . . . then another, and another . . . and then I knew the difference between a forest and a jungle.

From all around now there came sounds of crashings and of bushes being uprooted by other unseen elephants—and there, in front of us, five elephants—rather larger than life they seemed.

These five were quieter than the rest—vaguely conscious of something strange in their midst—often staring for long periods in the direction of our platform. We stayed as still as stone.

Then suddenly a puff of evening air gave one of them our wind. . . . Wheeling with surprising agility, he dashed off back into the undergrowth, confirming the half-formed suspicions of three others. I never thought elephants could, or would, move so quickly—and I was glad I was up in a large tree.

A great head and a pair of tusks. . . .

Note: This picture is of special interest. The dark patch that shows behind the eye of this Bull Elephant is a discharge from a small gland. When this gland operates the animal is in rut.

We were left with one big fellow who couldn't quite make up his mind. He stood facing us, ears and trunk upraised to catch the smallest sound or the faintest smell, for what seemed a very long time. He was never quite convinced that anything was wrong—or quite certain that everything was right—and when eventually he moved, he moved very slowly, hesitating at every cautious step to think again.

Breathlessly, we watched him going closer and closer, step by step, to where we knew there was a black cotton and a hidden camera. . . . It was a completely fascinating performance. . . . After interminable halts and decisions as to a variety of routes—it happened. . . . Night had almost fallen as he touched the trip-wire with his great broad forehead—a blinding flash, a terrified and terrifying squeal, a wild retreat and stampede into some bushes, and then dead silence. It all happened so close I even heard the tiny familiar click made by the shutter and I knew that a picture had been taken. An elephant had seen the light. He stood for hours in that clump of bushes trying to puzzle it all out—a very astonished animal—and when eventually he went, I never heard him go.

And then it was night and the glowworms came out with their own flashlights.

For a long time we lay and listened. There was plenty to listen to. Several elephants were down there in the water hole, blowing, snorting, gurgling, and generally making those sort of intimate noises that one usually reserves for moments of privacy—and the rest were crashing about happily somewhere in the neighbourhood.

And after a little, as the moon was not yet up, we must have dozed off to the sound of mighty washings and the noises of the crickets. I remember one particular cricket, just overhead, which kept up a consistent high pitched whine, similar to the sound one hears in an electric power station.

. . . it happened

Within a very short while we were both awakened by sounds, very little sounds, coming from directly below our tree. Peering over the edge of the platform I saw the huge grey shape of an elephant standing right below us—his back only about ten feet below. He was quietly examining various bits of wood we had cut during the building of our platform—picking up this and that with his trunk and then letting it fall again. Had I been Johnny Weismuller or Tarzan, or even Sabu, it would have been the easiest thing in the world to slip over the edge and drop down onto that broad back. . . . But as it was, I was only me, and I stayed where I was.

Later in the night, when the moon had risen, I again became conscious of small sounds. It was a bright moon and one could see quite well, and after a little I spotted what it was that was making the noises. In a tree, not thirty yards away, I could see small shapes scuttling up the trunk and out along the branches. Ah, thought I, monkeys . . . and I settled down to watch them.

I was leaning on one elbow with my face not twelve inches from one of the three trunks of our tree . . . and as I watched there suddenly took place one of the most terrifying things that has ever happened to me. I don't much mind frightening things that have an explanation, but things that happen suddenly without explanation are horrid.

From the top of the tree I was watching, a small black square detached itself from a high branch and came at me. And as it came through the air—sailing wierdly through the forest, the black square grew larger and larger. For one wild moment I thought I was dreaming again and that Gander would merely have some new phantasy to report to me in the morning—but Gander was sleeping. . . . And then, I'm afraid, panic set in. With the thing only about six yards away and coming, bigger and bigger, straight at my face—I ducked and covered my head with my arms. . . . Frightful thoughts raced through my mind of monster bats and Dracula and strange unknown things—and I remember expecting at any moment to be hit and enveloped in something cold and clammy. It was a very poor moment.

As it was . . . all that happened was that I heard a light tap on the tree trunk right beside my head—a scuffle of feet, and then nothing more. . . . Cautiously I uncovered my head from my arms and looked up . . . and there, within arm's reach was an animal looking at me. For about five seconds we looked at one another in wild astonishment and then there was a scuttle and a scurry and it went off the tree like a flash of lightning.

Slowly it dawned on me what I was witnessing.

I woke Gander and for the next hour we were entertained to a perfect midnight matinée—a moonlight circus performance —with flying foxes all around us, gliding miraculously from tree to tree—using our's as a sort of central trapeze so that we had the most perfect view.

There were about seven large trees, including our own, that formed the arena and about six foxes did the round of these trees. Scuttling straight to the top of one they would run out to the end of the high branches, pause, and then launch themselves into the air. With all four legs widespread and tail spread out, with the skin webbing between fore and hind legs stretched taut to form a square sail (about eighteen to twenty inches square ) they would come planing down in a long swooping glide to end with perfect timing, in a slight upward stall, on the trunk of another tree about fifteen to twenty-five feet above the ground. Then they would scuttle to the top of that tree and launch themselves off to the next—and so on, endlessly—all around us.

Flights would vary from about fifty to two hundred and fifty feet in length, and perhaps more. Six times they landed on our tree, right by our faces, and they appeared quite unperturbed by our presence. Once I had overcome my initial

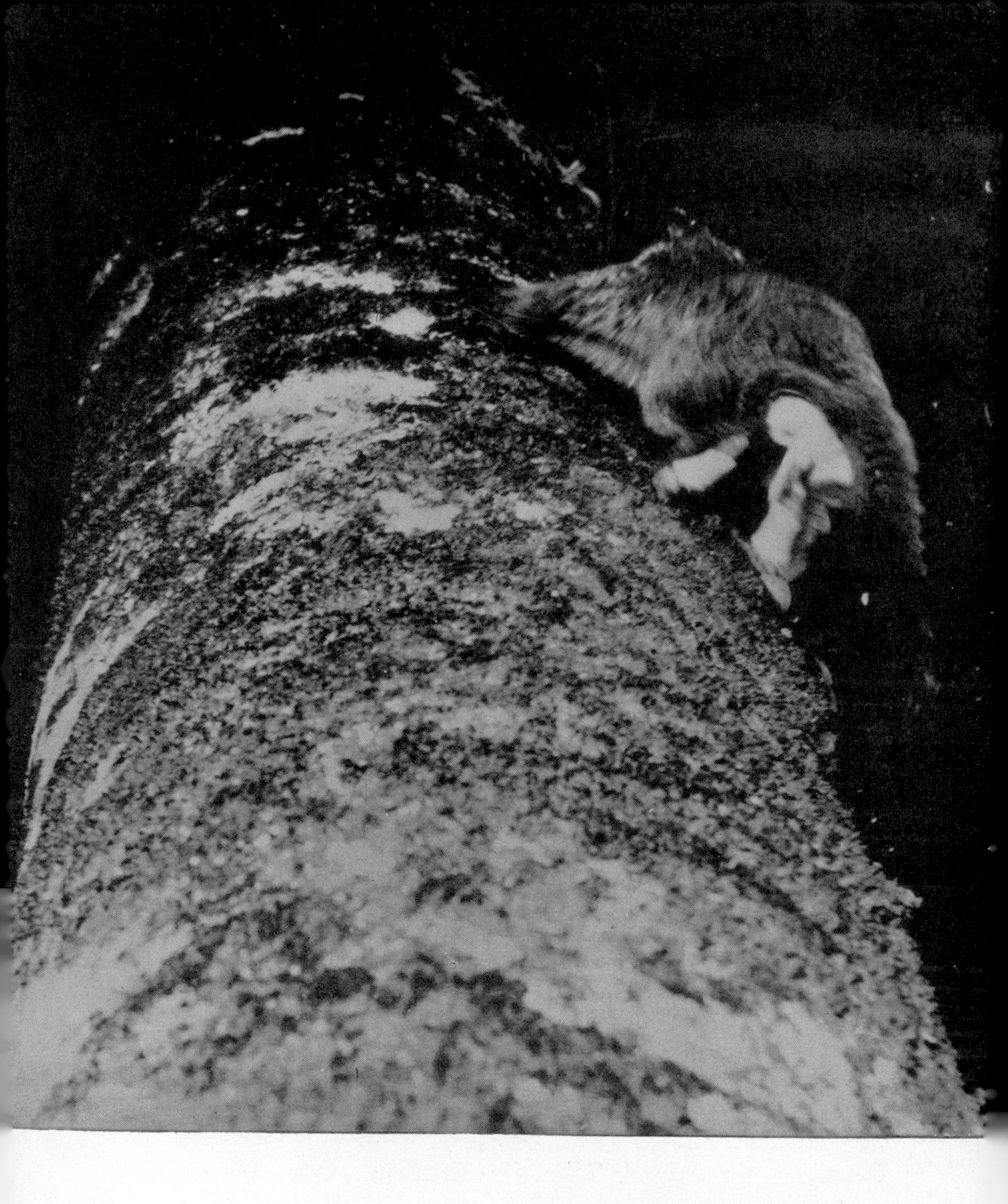

He landed on the tree trunk 12 inches from my head. FLYING FOX

fright, which was considerable, we set about trying to take a picture of them in the air coming towards us. We failed to get them actually in the air as it was too dark to see anything through the small Leica viewfinders, but I did succeed in getting one on the tree trunk right over my head just as it had landed.

And so, for about an hour, we had the most beautiful and perfect view of these animals, and we must have seen about fifty to seventy flights. It was only the next day that Colonel Hoier told us how very lucky we were to have seen what we did see. In all his time in the Congo he had only seen flying foxes once—and he never knew they were noctural as well as diurnal.

But I still wish the first one hadn't flown straight at me.

Later in the night there was a low snarl . . . a soft loping pitter patter of padded feet passing below the tree at a gentle trot. . . . Peering down I saw a grey shadow passing between the bushes—another low growl . . . and the next morning there was leopard spoor below the tree.

I watched the light come back to the forest at dawn. Bush buck were making their curious dog-like bark quite close and the flying foxes came out again to play.

At eight o'clock Njoki and the boys came back and it was all over. . . .

That morning I wrote in my diary. . . . "Last night combined all things—beauty and mystery and magic, and excitement and fear—and it was, I think, about as close as one can reasonably get to the animals and to the forest. We were part of that world. I shall never forget it. It was quite perfect."

*  *  *

HYAENA. His melancholy noise kept us awake at night.

# CHAPTER XI: THE ANTS

During our various travels about the countryside to discover all we could on the subject of gorillas, Gander and I took time out at Rwindi Camp in the hope of entangling a giant forest hog in our trip wires.

The Rwindi-Rutshuru section of the Park is mostly plains country which stretches east up to the frontier of Uganda and which, to the west rises to a mere six thousand five hundred feet. Nevertheless, although it cannot compare with the Volcano country, it is, true to Congo form, dramatic enough in one way or another. The Rutshuru and Rwindi Rivers together with seven hot springs at May-ya-Moto, most of which are actually boiling, provide plenty in the way of interest. On the plains, amid the Euphorbia and Thorn bushes, there are large herds of antelope and buffalo and elephant with a generous sprinkling of lion and other carnivora to ensure, according to the Laws of the Wild, that the numbers of the herds of antelope do not get out of hand. On the mud banks of the Rutshuru River the hippos are so thick they practically lie on top of one another.

We went to work on the giant forest hog down by the banks of the Rwindi River which flowed, not far away from camp, along down into Lake Edward. It was a hot, dusty and dismal place in which to do our work—and there was a mass of insect life and crawling things that was forever swarming up our legs, making light of the barriers of shorts and pants, and biting us in delicate places. There were also plenty of larger animals down there in the bush and in the reeds by the river bank, but spoor was much harder to interpret on the hard and dusty mud-caked ground. On several occasions we found ourselves cornered by elephants that had wandered into our midst and we had to down tools hurriedly and, leaving our cameras unset, moved out by any back door left open to us.

We lived during this period in one of the several bandas* provided for visitors to Rwindi Camp itself, and every night we went to sleep, as best we could, to the sounds of lions roaring and hyenas howling quite close by. One night we were turned out of our banda by an avalanche of ants that suddenly descended on us. Safari ants go straight across country and will brook no obstacle. Our banda was apparently dead on this particular expedition's compass course, and so they went through it and over it and round it and under it. We woke up at about midnight to find ants everywhere—in the roof, on the floor, all over the mosquito nets, in the beds, and even in the clothing inside our luggage. We woke up Njoko who was sleeping in the car outside and for about twenty minutes three of us carried on an uneven battle with fifty million ants. I have never seen such fixity of purpose—those ants were going somewhere and, whether this hut was in the way or not, they were on their way and that was that. Heaven knows how many we killed with flit guns and fly swatters and practically any other

* *Round, native-type mud huts with conical straw-thatched roofs.*

The most powerful jaws of any animal. HYAENA HEAD.

weapon that came to hand, but in the end the tide of ants was too much for us and we had to abandon home and shelter, and everything in it, until the following day.

So we had the two ends of the scale—in the daytime we were subject to eviction from our area by elephants and in the night-time we were liable to be turned out of our hut by ants.

What with one thing and another, the ants, the elephants, the sultry heat, the lions and hyenas and several sleepless nights, combined with trying to do delicate work with black cotton in the boiling heat of the noon-day sun, we soon became more than merely tired. It was one of those times when, no matter how hard you try, things never seem to go right. Two tired people, setting cameras together, soon found they were working slower than usual, and they tended to become impatient and disbelieving of one another's efficiency. The effect it had on me was that I became very pompous and intolerant and I was firmly convinced that unless I did everything myself, nothing at all would ever get done properly. It is unfortunate that whenever I get pompous and intolerant I nearly always make an ass of myself. This time it took the form of telling Gander how hopelessly clumsy he was being and then blundering in quick succession into three trip-wires and taking three unnecessary pictures of myself. The performance seemed to give great pleasure to Gander and Njoki.

I did my best to curb my impatience by day, but the trouble was that nothing could stop me talking in my sleep. . . . For what it is worth, and I don't know how much to believe him, Gander told me one morning—following on a poor night's rest and a trying day—that I had delivered myself of yet another noctural monologue. This time it was, "It's a pig!" Pause—and grumbling—then, urgently. . . . "It's a pig in the path!" Long pause—more grumbling—then, in very disgruntled tones . . . "Hell, Gander—*I* could have taken *ten* pictures by now. . . . "

But one was always at a disadvantage with Gander if one became pompous and impatient. He would just look at you and laugh, and you would find he was enjoying it all immensely —and, however hard you tried, it was damned hard to carry on being pompous.

We had some wonderful sessions with our old friends, the hippos. One day, when the elephants had been quite firm about our camera area, we went down to the banks of the Rutshuru River and wandered about with cameras on our own. It was the most tropical-looking river I had yet seen, fairly fast flowing and fringed with palms, winding its way through the most lovely setting. Hippos were to be seen pretty well everywhere one looked. We stalked up one one sun-bathing party of about twelve until we were very close and we spent about twenty minutes watching them and taking photographs. They are lovely impossible-looking animals, hippos, so contented and peaceful—until they suddenly stand up and stare straight at you.

I got up to within a few yards of one that was lying in the water. I took a photograph. He heard the click of the shutter and looked round. I took another photograph. He crash dived and I wasn't quick enough to get him doing so.

Further along we saw and counted thirty-three hippos lying out on a mud bank. Some were lounging around in deflated collapsed attitudes, like people in clubs, right out on the banks; others were half in and half out of the water, like people at Blackpool and Coney Island, lying higgledy-piggledy in amorous little groups more-or-less one on top of the next, all very sleepy and contented; and one or two lay out in the water, like Colonel Blimp at the baths, almost totally submerged, just letting the river go by and occasionally lifting a nostril or two out to blow a bit. The whole scene represented a very reasonable attitude towards life, and it made me almost want to go down and join in with them.

We had some wonderful sessions with our old friends the Hippos.

(1) I crept up close to one and took a picture. . . .
(11) . . . he heard the click of the camera and looked round. . . .

In the Aberdare Mountains our main difficulties with the cameras had been wind and rain and monkeys and bloody-minded partridges. Here at Rwindi they were heat, elephants, ants, beetles, and me. There was seldom a day passed without elephants either preventing us reaching our cameras at all or else blundering into trip-wires set for more reasonably sized animals. Ants and beetles were forever swarming into and round the cameras. The former somehow generally managed to short the batteries and were very apt to lay eggs and gubbins all over the works. The latter seemed to appreciate an apparently succulent, but essential, piece of wood we used inside the synchroniser.

However, in spite of everything, we had our reward. When the negatives taken at Rwindi had been flown back to Nairobi from Kampala and developed, "Weary" Wood sent us a cable congratulating us on three really good pictures of giant forest hog.

Here again I believe I am right in saying that these were the first successful pictures ever to be taken of this animal at large. As with the Bongo, we had been lucky again.

* * *

We got him by day. . . . Giant Forest Hog

And we got him again by night. GIANT FOREST HOG

# CHAPTER XII: THE PROBLEM

Before leaving England we had read pretty well all we could find on the subject of gorillas—and we had imagined a great deal more. Ever since we had been in Africa, and particularly in the Congo, we had questioned everyone, black, white, and khaki, who had any claim at all to any knowledge, however expert or slight, of the Great Ape and his habits. As soon as we got to the Congo, we found that most of our armchair information was considered speculative rather than hard fact. And yet the longer we stayed in the Congo and listened to the I-know-what-I'm-talking-about-because-I've-seen-it-happen people who lived there, we found that each new bit of information conflicted with the last.

After about a month, among other things, we had collected the following information:—

1. That gorillas are very difficult to locate and find.
2. That gorillas are all too easy to locate and find.
3. That gorillas never follow game trails through the forests.
4. That gorillas always follow game trails through the forests.

5. That gorillas never sleep twice in the same place.

6. That gorillas often sleep in the same place.

7. That gorillas often raid the native shambas for maize etc.

8. That they do no such thing.

9. That they are very aggressive and charge at sight.

10. That they are scared to hell of man and run away immediately.

11. That they frequently climb trees.

12. That they never climb trees.

13. That you can drive gorillas.

14. That you can't.

And a whole lot more in like vein. . . . There are entire pages of my diary giving similar facts. Every time we got information from the natives and the pygmies they contradicted themselves over and over again. Whereas with Africans this is nothing very new, and is certainly not restricted to the subject of gorillas alone, we nevertheless came to the conclusion eventually, rightly I think, that nothing very much *is* known about the gorilla and his behaviour, and that the sooner we got one or two facts, straight from the gorilla's mouth, the better.

We subsequently had several encounters with gorillas and it did not take us very long to realise the magnitude of the problem we had set ourselves. Gorillas are not easy animals to photograph.

I should hate anyone to consider the following observations on these animals in any scientific light. It ought by this time in any case to be quite clear to the reader that we were not two scientists.

To begin with the gorilla is a very large animal, and, even if one supposes him not aggressive, he is at least well capable of being so. The big grey-back male can run to as much as four hundred pounds in weight, and his size and strength when in his prime are more than impressive. . . . When he stands upright, which he very rarely does (and generally it is either only to get a better view or to beat his chest) he reaches six feet, and with arms spread wide he can stretch nine feet from finger-tip to finger tip. He measures about a yard across the shoulders and better than two yards round the chest, and his biceps and forearms are sufficiently strong for him to be able to break a heavy rifle in two without bothering to use a knee to help.

All this makes him quite a customer.

But surely, so runs the argument in one's head, even in view of all these things, it is better to be confronted by a gorilla than by anything so huge and powerful as an elephant? Maybe it is—maybe an elephant can be more dangerous. . . . But the fascinating and frightening thing about going after gorillas is that here you are confronting yourself with something that is not only immensely strong and unpredictable, but also with something that is built in much the same form as a human being—and that you and he may even have come from the same original mould. It is this that gives one an uncanny feeling down the spine as you struggle around in those fantastic forests—that here, all around you, are things that are dangerous and strange, and yet that there is possibly only some tiny, unknown, missing thread between you and those things, preventing mutual comprehension.

I see I keep laying myself open to criticism, and even ribald jokes—but I do it deliberately. . . . You cannot have these feelings and sensations in zoos, but out in the forests, confronted by a family of gorillas; mother, father and the children, you very definitely can. I had the feeling over and over again that here was something one ought to be able to understand . . . that here were things that possibly, way back in the mists of prehistoric time, we may well have been able to understand . . . that here was a case of one thing taking to one way of life and a similar thing taking to another, resulting in a wide gulf forming between the two—and, upon my word, I don't know which one of us was really the better chooser.

Of the two, man and gorilla, the latter is certainly the more peaceful. He lives a simple life in a beautiful and endlessly productive world. He can, and does, live in apparently complete harmony with elephant and buffalo and lion and he harms none of the other weaker neighbours in the forest world. And . . . Oh, well . . . I hesitate to take the matter further.

And yet, when you look for gorillas you cannot help but have this strange uncanny fear of the nearly comprehensible unknown—you get it the first time you see the imprint of a huge hand in the mud. Human or sub-human the gorilla is in a different class. He is not like other animals. He is somehow a vagrant savage—a kind of Meanderthal man if you like. . . .

But so far as we and our cameras were concerned, the difficulties were immense. The forests were thick and tangled and dark, and the only places where there was space for "depth" to a photograph were in the trails made by elephant and buffalo. All the other animals regularly make use of these trails, but it is only very rarely that the gorilla bothers about them at all.

The gorillas travel about the forests in bands—each band generally a family. They wander where they will, without any apparent plan, feeding as they go on bamboo shoots and wild celery, and they seldom spend more than a day in any one given area. As the forests are almost endless, and the supply of celery extremely plentiful, it is often very difficult to locate these family bands at all, and next to impossible to predict the direction of their future movements. Furthermore, being a vegetarian, he will not come, as will the leopard and the lion, to a kill.

Unlike you and me, who have to follow game trails, or else spend hours hacking our way with pangas yard by yard through the forests, the gorilla has no such difficulty. He seldom, if ever, follows any track and his great strength and

Gorilla Food. Wild celery.

Gorilla Bed. A typical "nest" made by a gorilla—showing fresh droppings

shaggy coat allow him to push his way quite easily through stuff that appears impenetrable.

He and his family will go to considerable trouble each evening to building themselves comfortable beds in the shape of great round nests, but it is of little use to hang around a group of these nests for they practically never use the same beds two nights running.

True he does go down quite often to raid the native shambas but at the edge of the forests there are many of these "gardens" and there is no knowing when he will come, or where. . . . The gorilla is the vagabond par excellence—the happy wanderer with nothing to fear and nothing to lose. But you can find him and his family—quite easily sometimes. The only snag is that he will not wait around for you to do complicated things with cameras and trip-wires.

Generally speaking a gorilla will not, unlike certain other animals, attack a man without some kind of provocation. He has to be surprised or disturbed or driven before he will charge. But then he will charge. . . . There are some people who hold that his first one or two charges are bluff, in the hope of scaring you away, and although we witnessed this maneuver, I was never too certain that each charge was not going to develop into the real thing. . . . And if and when the real thing does occur, you need a heavy rifle in your hands.

And yet, to approach one of these gorilla bands, or to study them, let alone to take photographs of them, involves disturbing them. When you approach, their first instinct is to retire in the opposite direction; when you follow them up, their second reaction is generally to show, in very easily understood terms, that they don't approve of being followed; if you persist, they cope with the matter.

On top of all this there was, as I have already explained, our solemn undertaking with Brussels neither to kill nor be killed by a gorilla, and to undertake no action that would be liable to lead to either.

I suppose it would be a relatively easy matter to advance right up to a gorilla with two fully armed Commandos, one on either side of you with Tommy guns, and to take its photograph with a flashlight press camera just before or during the inevitable charge. But it would hardly be a natural photograph of a gorilla at large. It would be a picture of an extremely angry gorilla just about to die. And furthermore there would probably be a mass of tangled foliage and undergrowth between the lens and the gorilla.

After we had been to Luberu and Tchibinda and Mikeno and had investigated all three gorilla areas, Gander and I began to wonder whether, failing some blind fluke, forty men with four hundred cameras and four thousand miles of black cotton might not be more to the point.

Meanwhile, visiting these various and widely spaced area involved a deal of travel, and travel in the Congo is not without originality.

* * *

HIGH UP IN GORILLA LAND. The problem was—where on earth to put a trip wire. . . .

Baboons are good pedestrians.

# CHAPTER XIII: THE ROAD

The more I write of this book, the more I wish I could go back to those places about which I am writing—and the more I wish I had it in me to explain in words just why.

With so much to write about, of the so many things that were of interest to me, it is difficult for me to sort the wheat from the chaff and to avoid being long-winded. I constantly remind myself of the man who wrote a very long letter to a friend and ended it by saying, "I apologise for writing you such a long letter—I'm afraid I hadn't time to write a short one."

My difficulty is that I have the time, quantities of it now that I am back in civilian life again, but somehow the ability to be short and concise appears to be lacking.

Pedestrians in the street traffic often act like baboons. Baboons, on the other hand, make extremely good pedestrians. If you are driving along and you come across, as you may well do in Africa, a troop of baboons in the roadway, one gentle toot on the horn is all that is required for a complete and instantaneous evacuation. With the natives themselves, on certain unfrequented tracks, we found that the reactions were much the same—only perhaps not so efficiently carried out. There was with the natives more of a tendency to panic than with the baboons.

The first reaction was to drop all bundles, however precious, right in the middle of the track, and then to run like hell in all directions, across country, o'er hill and dale, through bush and thicket, until they were practically out of sight, and hearing of the road. Such apprehension could only come from one of two things—either from the unfamiliarity of the motor car which was still a menacing monster, or else, it was all too familiar, and they had had some experience of its capabilities at the hands of someone like *le brave* Commandant Hubert. . . . In either case I'm afraid we always rather looked forward to meeting a party of natives on the more remote tracks. Apart from the delaying action of the discarded bundles we generally had to stop as we were helpless with laughter. There was one little black man, I remember, who ran like a hare down the road in front of us, arms and legs flying as though all the hounds of hell were after him. He ran for at least half a mile before it occurred to him that he would be more successful across country, and we couldn't even get past him to stop all the unnecessary exercise.

But once the native becomes accustomed to the motor car and to some sort of less energetic Highway Code, he becomes an inveterate car rider. If ever one went anywhere in the truck one could always guarantee that a number would swarm on to the back and ride with you—no matter how inconvenient the direction. Inside the station wagon the driving mirror always seemed to reflect a mass of eager black faces crowding up close behind the driver's seat urging the driver to rush at and run over any animal that appeared on the road. They seemed to regard, and even the sophisticated Njoki was in on this, the motor car as a wonderful instrument invented by the white man for providing unexpected menus for the black man.

I only killed one thing in Africa and that was a hare I ran over one day by mistake. My popularity went up to unexpected heights.

Our truck was always considered very favourably because of the great wooden construction we had had erected on the back to hold on all our goods and chattels. They used to climb up this as high as they could, shouting and whooping in the wind, until we looked more like a travelling circus act than anything else. Sometimes it was almost too much fun.

The main road that ran from the frontier to Lake Kivu had as surface for the last twenty miles or so only volcanic ash and lava, and this was pretty hard on tires—but it was a road. It became famous with us for a particular stretch where for a few miles it ran through the forests of the National Albert Park at the foot of Mount Mikeno. We often had to travel through there by night and at night time elephants considered that the roadway belonged to them.

The road that ran from Goma round the east side of Lake Kivu down to Costermansville could scarcely have been called a road. On one occasion it took us more than ten hours to do a hundred and fifty miles on this road, and how we ever managed to average nearly fifteen miles an hour is still a mystery to me. Neither of us, however, in the least resented the time we spent on that long and tiring drive because it was such an unusual driving experience and practically an adventure all by itself.

One starts out bravely from Goma on something resembling a road and pretty soon this develops into a track—and not long afterwards into something rather less than a footpath. From then on one runs over every kind of novel surface from rocks and mud and general hillside to what appear to be good grassy lawns. For at least seventy miles of the way it isn't possible to pass any vehicle or to overtake anything, and for this reason there is a local law that it is one-way one day and the other the next—but this is barely necessary for if two cars meet in one day it is considered big stuff. This "road" ranges somewhere between the four thousand foot mark and ten thousand feet above sea level and at times you arrive at places where you feel you are in an aeroplane and not a car. There are hairpin bends and precipices and places where rocks and boulders fall, and there are forests and wild uplands and staggering views. Bridges, when they are necessary, which is quite often, are tree trunks lashed together, and it is not unusual to do a three mile detour to gain a hundred yards. For the whole distance of one hundred and fifty miles one passes no house, and if you break down or run out of petrol—well . . . that's just too bad. The only signs of human life we saw were the odd groups of natives walking along with their bundles on their heads—and whenever we met them we had the same devastating stampede and flight.

By now I expect it is a fine metalled road that has been travelled over by many an army truck, but I hope to heaven it is still the same as it was.

Even at that time sensible people used generally to go from Goma to Costermansville by the lake steamer which travelled up and down the lake once weekly, and put their vehicle on board as well. But this boat too was unusual in several ways—the principal one being that it floated the very reverse way to an iceberg—one fifth in the water and four-fifths out. The addition of a vehicle on deck produced a result that really required a distress signal at the masthead.

Wherever we went, we always gravitated back to Goma. After being out for a period it was always a pleasure to come back to the little Hotel des Volcans, which stood practically on the lake shore not far from where Nyamlagira poured her stream of lava into Kivu, and there to have a proper bed and a bath and a meal cooked by someone other than Njoki. In this little hostel we found, of all things, a ping-pong table. The

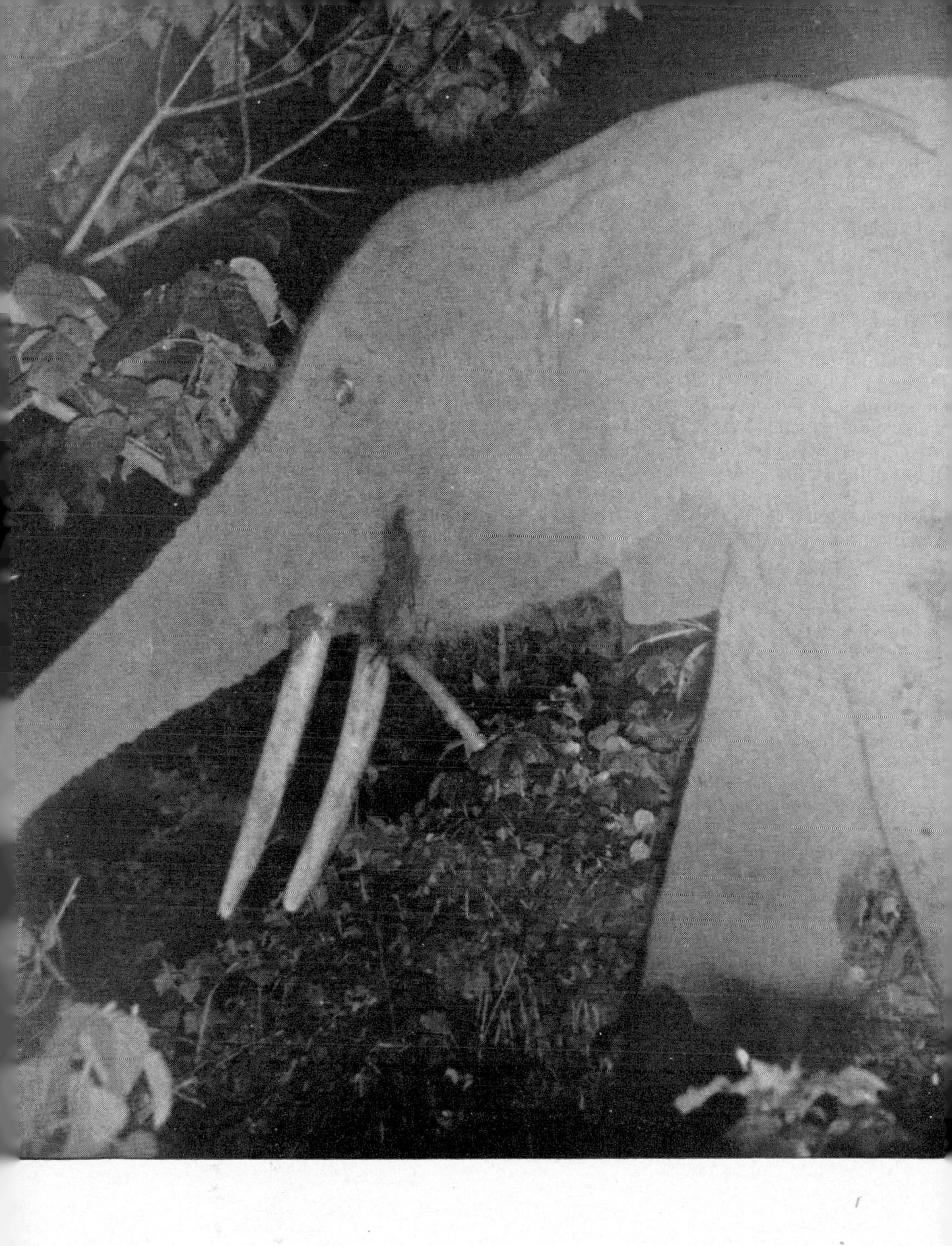

Elephants are generally photogenic, but sometimes our results were unflattering. . . .

. . . and sometimes the subject himself was suspiciously cock-eyed.

main article of furniture in Gander's sitting room in his home in London was always a ping-pong table—and so the struggle to be Champion of Kensington merely continued under the new name of the Congo Championship.

We went to Goma to collect mail and to write letters. Mail was always an unknown quantity and the Congo postal services, such as they were, always seemed to conspire against us. And when we did get letters, they required a good deal of collecting of thought on our part because there was generally some confusion going on at home about the production of the revue. We also went there to replenish our supplies of food and fuel for the next effort in the forests, to get clean and tidy (but never to shave, for we were proud of our beards) and to read last month's newspapers—and for me to talk to someone other than Gander, and vice versa. We were never there very long, but when we were it was good.

In general there were always very few white people about and not often cars on the roads. There were the few regulars—the hotel and store owners, the Belgian administrators, the White Fathers from the mission at Lulengu and the occasional visitor. We met Field Marshal Smuts one time, travelling through with Colonel Denys Reitz, the ex-High Commissioner for South Africa in London, who has since unfortunately died. Colonel Reitz was a great lover of wild animals and I should have loved to have shown him the results of our photography.

On the road, traveling from place to place, there was always something to look at. If it wasn't the volcanoes it was the natives; if it wasn't the natives it was the animals; if it wasn't the animals it was something else. Once we saw two lions quite close to the roadside. Close to the lions were eight elephants standing together in the open. They were in a circle with their heads together looking as though they were waiting for scrum-half to put the ball in. We had a lovely view of them when they presently moved off down the hill half towards us.

The swinging flexibility of their trunks always seems extraordinary—and the gait which appears easy and loping is curiously awkward in the forelegs. They stopped half way down the hill and two males had a minor sparring match over a female. We thought for one moment that we were going to witness something really big in the way of eternal triangles, but they very soon, and very sensibly, became bored with the whole thing and wandered contentedly on.

One may be able to travel very fast on the modern highway in the civilized world, but all the highways and metalled roads of Europe and America are poor stuff compared with the bumpy roads of Africa.

* * *

two of them had a minor sparring match.

# CHAPTER XIV: DON'T LOOK 'ROUND NOW . . .

It became very exhausting at each new place we visited to explain at length to countless strangers exactly what we were up to and what it was we wanted. When we got to Luberu we had a very long and confused conversation in a form of French with the local District Commissioner. This was not made easier as the first part of the conversation was held in a large barn-like building where he was at the time holding a court of law, and some two hundred natives formed an interesting but embarrassing audience. He couldn't be made to believe that we had all the necessary permits to go after gorillas and he kept on repeating like a very overheated parrot, "*C'est contre la loi, à cause des accidents.*" The more he banged the table, the more the natives thought that we were two law breakers who were going to share their jail with them that night.

We managed however to get things straight, or straight enough, and finally, with a sigh of relief, we pushed off to find what we could find. From Luberu itself we drove, together with a native who was said to know the gorilla country well,

GORILLA TRAIL. Gorillas went through the bamboos here and left this trail of their passing.

some thirty kilometres back down (up and down to be more exact), until we came to a rest camp at the edge of the Reserve. This consisted of one miserable little mud house in a small and somewhat smelly native village called Kibonda and here we unpacked the cars and stayed.

We had been told in Brussels that there had been some trouble at Luberu and that the gorillas there were disturbed, but we didn't know to what this was due. Once there we found that there was considerable ill feeling between the natives of our small village and the gorillas in the forests around them. The trouble was that the gorillas were conducting fairly regular raids on the local shambas or cultivation and stealing and destroying the crops—and there was, not unnaturally, considerable resentment over this. We visited and inspected several of the shambas that had suffered damage. There was one that had been raided earlier on that very morning we saw it and it could better, or perhaps only, have been described as a shambles. Everywhere the maize was trampled down and torn up by the roots. The gorillas evidently liked corn on the cob as much as I do.

The trouble was, so far as our plans were concerned, that one could never tell which area of cultivation was going to be visited next, nor from which direction the raid would come. Hunting with rifles, it would have been a comparatively easy proposition, but hunting with trip wires, no.

Every now and again the natives of an area that is having gorilla trouble will band together and go forth, law or no law, in mass against the gorilla. They go with spears, long eight or nine foot affairs, and, when they find him, they advance in lines on the gorilla—the front line crouching and the rear line, close behind, standing. The rear rank uses its spears in orthodox fashion launching them from the shoulder, but the front line holds its weapons low, at a narrow angle to the ground, with the sharp ends pointing upwards and the rear

) trip wires con-
cted to two cam-
as allowed a will-
g Hippo. . . .

(11) to take his picture from both front and rear.

ends trailing in the mud. When they get the gorilla to charge, he impales himself on a line of spears which dig back into the ground when he strikes them and thus remain firm—while from above this line he receives a volley from those standing up.

Not more than a year before we arrived in the Congo, the natives had openly declared war on the gorillas and in one big round-up they had killed twenty-three of them in this fashion. The story does not relate what the gorillas' score was in natives . . . but the whole affair caused no end of consternation to the Belgian Administration, and the local District Commissioner was still smarting from some of the rockets still being shot at him from Brussels. That was why he couldn't understand how we had got permits.

We did a lot of tramping up and down game trails and crawling through thick jungle and we saw a lot of things—but no gorilla. Then one day we found spoor—very fresh spoor it looked—and droppings too. The spoor showed clearly both hand and foot marks quite deeply imprinted in the mud, and it looked surprisingly large—particularly the thumb (or should I say big toe?) Later on we found nests . . . and at one point we could even smell the animals, so they could not have been very far away. But, although we followed up, we saw no sign of them and heard them make no sound.

One morning we woke up and Gander had just informed me of that night's utterance. . . . It appears that this time I had only spoken once, in very hushed tones.

"The buffaloes came by quite close yesterday." and that was all. He was very disappointed, because he rather liked to join in the conversation to see what I would say next, but this time that was all I was prepared to give away.

We began to move around in a desultory manner making vague and slightly helpless plans for fresh attempts to make contact with gorillas somewhere in the wild and endless forests that surrounded us. It was one of those dismal needle-in-the-haystack mornings. A period of conversation with some indifferent natives in no particular language seemed to make things a lot more difficult. I was beginning to wonder if we should ever find gorillas.

Half an hour later one of our boys came in and reported that we could indeed find them and there were some at that moment not ten minutes away in the forest. This was a fairly frequent practice in the mornings and, in Africa, even the most hopelessly enthusiastic become accustomed to this kind of statement from natives employed and paid by them. However, largely on account of the fact that we could think of nothing more constructive to do at the moment, and because breakfast was not yet ready, we decided to go off and investigate.

We had with us the boy we had brought from Luberu, one other moderately respectable local and one very ugly little man wearing practically no clothes at all. The latter two were armed with spears. From force of habit rather than anything else we armed ourselves with Leica cameras—and off we went, the natives confident, and we doubting greatly. Njoki was still busy preparing breakfast and humming some doleful tune to himself.

We came, in a very few minutes, to a small hill, thickly wooded. By this time our party had mysteriously swelled to about seven or eight—more tough little black men wearing practically no clothes and each armed with a spear. We didn't bother about them. Then somebody said, "There they are," and we all stopped. We looked and saw nothing. Chimpanzees perhaps, we thought—but certainly not gorillas—not before breakfast anyway. . . . We moved on a few yards until we were on a little clear hillock and then we stopped again.

This time there was no room for doubt. . . . *There were gorillas* . . . right bang in view—about two hundred feet away. . . . And I don't care what anybody says, Martin Johnson, Carl

It was difficult always to get exposures right. ELAND

Akeley or the first gorilla to learn how to speak, but these gorillas were fifty to sixty feet up in trees.

Everything seemed to happen very slowly, and we were both aware rather vaguely and in trancelike fashion that photography was indicated—so we took two or three pictures —dreamlike efforts.

Shortly after this the animals became aware of our presence. There were four of them up there in the trees. I was watching the biggest one, high up. He was folding his arms across a branch as a sort of pillow for his head and he looked just like an old man resting. And then the next moment he came down that tree, not like you and I come down trees, but head first, like a flash of lightning, and not at all like an old man. He disappeared through the feathery tops of the bamboos which were below us—and then various parts of the bamboo forest, where the others were as well, began swaying about and crashing sounds emerged.

And then we heard the first bark of alarm—half bark and half roar—a terrible, staccato, frightening sound, very loud and sudden, and obviously coming from something with an outsize pair of lungs and chest.

I shall probably receive a number of protests from learned and experienced sources pointing out that all this is nonsense because gorillas don't climb trees. I don't care. I can only report what I saw—and yet I should hate to include myself in among the many "I-know-what-I'm-talking-about-because-I've-seen-it-with-my-own-eyes" type of people, because generally they have no other argument than that.

For a little we watched and listened. By this time our party numbered nearly twenty. Where these savages came from, armed with great spears and dressed in practically nothing, we couldn't think. They simply came slipping out of nowhere and joined us. But they all saw the gorillas way up in the trees, and they all knew, only too well, that they really were gorillas.

We remembered later that there had been a lot of excitement and movement in the village of Kibonda that morning and more than the usual amount of jabberation . . . and the news had probably gone far and wide that there were gorillas in the neighbourhood and that there were two crazy white men who wanted to see them—come and join the fun sort of thing. News travels fast in the forests.

As soon as everything had quieted down a bit and it seemed that the gorillas had departed further afield, we expressed a wish to approach a little, to go down there into the thick undergrowth and the bamboos to find the spoor and look around. Twenty-five strong, and with no rifle, we entered the forest close to where we had last seen the animals.

Ten yards into the thick stuff and we were greeted with crashing sounds as of something big coming towards us, and then there came a fearful bellow from about fifty yards distance. Quite a different sound from the first bark of alarm—long drawn out and challenging, and, to my mind, since it was too thick to see the gorilla, infinitely more alarming. And there on the ground, below and round the big trees, was masses of spoor and fresh droppings. We stayed very quiet and examined everything. Fearing some sort of face-to-face business and a possible accident, and bearing in mind the very strict laws, the instinct was to retire and let bad alone, but the natives were keen on advancing. So, fondly imagining the gorillas would do the retiring, we advanced a little further, creeping as quietly as we could.

The next thing we knew was that there was a charge and an ear-splitting roar coming from not more than twelve yards away in the undergrowth. The gorilla had done some advancing as well, and was evidently coming closer. As a noise it is more or less indescribable, and I no longer scoff at anybody for dropping into "Boy's Life" language in attempting to put it

The Puff Adder is fortunately a slow mover, so it is possible to get quite close and take a picture by hand.

into words. It is about the most frightening thing one can imagine.

The moment it came the natives put up an answering roar —up went the spears and they ranged themselves in line for action. . . .

We suddenly tumbled to what was happening. These natives definitely wanted to get to grips with the gorilla and kill it. Our presence there was merely a glorious excuse for them to break the law and get away with it. For us, however, there would have been no getting away with it—it would have meant the end of our efforts in the Congo. And yet here was the extremely tricky situation of a line of tense and highly excited natives creeping forward inch by inch with a great barrier of spears—and there only about ten to twelve yards in front of them the bamboos and tangled undergrowth were swaying violently from one side to another as the gorilla gave vent to his wrath.

We yelled at them to come back, but they paid no attention—and it looked as though at any moment now we would either have one dead gorilla or several dead natives on our hands—that was, unless something happened pretty quickly.

There was only one thing to do. We had to get between them and the gorilla and force them back. So we did this—pushing and shouting at them and getting entangled in undergrowth and spears, until the line broke and one by one we got them back down to the track we had cut. . . . And all the time the bamboos and bushes just behind us were swaying and being ripped about and one had the dreadful feeling of "don't look 'round now but there's an extremely angry gorilla just over your right shoulder. . . ."

We never actually saw the gorilla at that range, but there wasn't much time to hang around—and there was too much at stake. We were entirely concentrated on the natives—and anyway the noise it was making was more than sufficient.

But we got them out . . . and this time we retreated quite a long way. And when it was all over I began to feel a little sick.

Back out in the open again we found that the noise had attracted even more natives from the nearby village and that the party now numbered nearly fifty. They were all in a very excited state—a miniature army of near-naked men with spears —and it was a job to calm them down and assure them that there was absolutely nothing further doing. Then, considerably shaken, we sat down for about twenty minutes and collected our wits and tried to make certain we were not dreaming. Afterwards we went back to camp, looking, in the middle of our group, much like prisoners of war in a native uprising.

When we got there Njoki was petulant because breakfast was cold.

So we eventually made contact with the gorillas, but instead of elucidating anything it merely produced yet another snag on top of all the others. How were we to get to work on the tricky business of photography if we could exercise so little control over the natives?

* * *

# CHAPTER XV: GOD

We split up once into two groups—each with ten cameras and Gander went off to try to get pictures of Sittatunga in the marshes near Kabale. I stayed on in the forests trying, in vain, for buffalo. I was camped only a few miles off the main Uganda-Kivu road and one day I came down out of the forests, got the car and drove myself to Lulengu. I did this because I wanted to visit the White Fathers who had a mission at Lulengu, and also because I hoped to replace a hat that I had stupidly mislaid and lost when going round the camera traps in the forest.

I had driven about six miles along the main road when I saw a curious object and stopped. It was my hat sitting perched on a stick by the side of the road. How it got there, I can't imagine, and I never solved the mystery. However, I continued, with my hat, to the Mission and here I introduced myself to the White Fathers as an Englishman who wanted to know what White Fathers did in missions.

They were as interested in me and what I was doing, as I was in them and we got along famously together. I was glad I had a beard to be in keeping with them all, but their beards were

He will carry almost anything for a penny a day.

long and white and silky whereas mine was brown and rather grubby and all over the shop.

The mission buildings were fine and there was even a football ground within the compound—and I learned a lot about the natives from the Fathers, who were very kind and hospitable. I had lunch with them, followed by coffee and cigars . . . which was a little surprising. After I had left I made some notes about my visit and what the White Fathers had told me—and this is what I wrote:—

"I learnt:—

1. That in the mission they deal with about four to five hundred native children at one time.

2. Like Hitler they catch them young, but

3. Unlike Hitler they teach them the mysterious manner in which God moves.

4. They also teach them elementary figures, writing, reading, geography and a certain amount of history.

5. Other classes include agriculture, manners, gymnastics, dress, singing, etc.

6. The main class, of course, is religion.

7. Ages run from six or seven-year-olds to fourteen and fifteen.

8. The bottom class learns how to count to five, and the top class that the world is round.

9. At the end of their time the pupils know area but not volume.

10. The natives have their own God. A lofty sort of person who created everything, white men and all, but who, rightly I thought, no longer has any interest in his creation.

11. They carve rather ugly little figures of this God.

12. They believe in the survival of the spirit in that when one of them dies he or she merely becomes a ghost. All departed ancestors are ghosts. These ghosts give them far more concern than their God.

13. Each family is concerned only with its own ghosts. When things go right they know the ghosts are good ghosts and so they offer up a cow or a goat as a bonus to them. When things go wrong (illness or bad harvest) they run to the village witch doctor who tells them that their ancestral ghosts are bad ghosts and that they must instantly offer up a cow or a goat to turn them into good ghosts.

14. There are several kinds of witch doctors—some primarily to distinguish between good and bad ghosts, some to bring rain, some to deal with the harvests, and presumably one or two on the local Stock Exchange.

15. The White Fathers make no attempt to suppress witch doctors—they proceed calmly and confidently with their own medicine. They 'leave it to the Government to forbid anything it considers too illogical.'

16. There is generally one hut set aside in each village, purely for the use and comfort of ancestral ghosts. It is always kept well stocked with food and offerings which quietly rot.

17. Except for periodic visits to their home villages, departed ancestors, or rather their spirits, go to two places:—

a) The ones who have been good go to Muhumvira (a pleasant place over the mountains), and
b) The ones who have been bad go into the crater of Nyamlagera volcano, and are kept very busy refueling the fires.

18. They do not consider that animals have spirits.

19. The White Fathers are doing away with all these beliefs and are teaching Christianity.

20. The mission deals with sickness. Main troubles are consumption, meningitis, fever and leprosy. The village between camp and Lulengu Mission is a leper colony."

Afterwards one of the White Fathers took me all round the buildings and showed me the class rooms. He gave me permission, when the holidays were over, to return and attend some of the classes and also to attend a Sunday service to hear the kids sing hymns. He also showed me some of the very rare efforts the children do at drawing. What they produce is unimaginative and generally some severely stylised design of a very simple nature.

After a very interesting time I thanked the White Fathers very much and drove back and went to my camp and my buffaloes.

I had always wanted to know who it was that went so far to put the little black men into trousers and shirts and collars and the little black girls into ugly frocks, and told them it was wrong to show their shimmering black bodies in the sun; and who it was who gave them so much to think about, and so many strange and useless things to think about at that, that sometimes the little black boys and girls even scarcely had the time left to do the thing that came most easily to them—to smile. . . . I had always wanted to know who they were, these African missionaries, and what they were like, and why they did it. And now I had been to a mission and met the missionaries and liked them very much—but I still wasn't clear as to why they did it.

* * *

# CHAPTER XVI: THE WAY UP

I am never very happy about mountains unless they have snow on them—and then I love them very dearly. Mountains that have rocky crags and precipices and are giddily perpendicular are beautiful to look at, but I prefer to look at them from below. Once I am forced to climb up rock faces or steep cliffs, I find I suffer from the thing called "vertigo." Gander had precisely the same trouble with mountains as I, but he, rather unkindly, called his trouble "funk."

The morning we started up Mount Mikeno was typical of all starts to adventures in Africa. Col. Hoier had very kindly arranged for the necessary porters who were to carry the kit for us and, on waking that morning, we heard the sound of many voices outside the hut. When we opened the door, we were confronted by faces—rows and rows of grinning black faces peering at us—and the air became thick with "Jambos."* We performed our toilets and ate our breakfasts to a fine

* *The native greeting.*

Preparations for Safari. Kasisi in charge of loading operations.

ON THE MOVE. . . . A motley collection of kit.

audience, and then the eternal business of packing the kit up began all over again.

From the crowd outside there gradually emerged twenty porters of odd sizes and even odder appearances. In charge of them was one named Kasisi, again provided by Colonel Hoier, a boy employed by the administration of the National Albert Park, and clad in the splendour of an old army overcoat and a red tarbush with the initials P.N.A. on his epaulettes. The remainder wore various bits of cloth strung here and there in haphazard fashion. Clothes inevitably make the man and Kasisi cashed in on his appearance by wielding a certain amount of authority. On these occasions Njoki, in all the finery of our own discarded garments, inevitably became insufferably superior and, with hired porters, he immediately acted the knowing "townee" coping with the simple minded country-cousin.

As soon as the tent and all the equipment were packed into various suitable bundles each porter seized the load he fancied—the quicker getting the smaller as usual—and then we all started up the track towards Mikeno in a long, long trail awinding—this time *to* and not *from* the mountain.

But it wasn't as easy as all that. It never was. It took a great deal of excitement and pushing and barging around and shouting before the caravan departed—and we ourselves did our usual share of forgetting and remembering and unpacking again to see if it really was there—but in the end, after a lot of fun had been had by all, we managed to be away shortly after nine o'clock. Two hours that would have sent Railway Express gray.

And then we started off through the Shambas towards Mikeno.

A certain portion of our food supply accompanied us on foot in the shape of a very engaging lamb on a string. There was also a chicken slung over one black shoulder, a large quantity of Colonel Hoier's vegetables somewhere else, some tinned

Elephant Trail. Elephant went this way last night and left the usual destruction.

Sometimes it was like a wild overgrown garden where everything grew.

food in a basket balanced on a black head and somewhere, heaven knew where, a dozen eggs.

It seems hardly fair these days to go into the matter of food and cost of living, but it is true that just before the war one could have lived like a millionaire in the Congo on a hundred pounds a year, for it was a land of plenty, both from the point of view of food and willing labour. To hire a porter for one day cost about one penny—and for that princely sum he was ready, and apparently anxious, to carry anything from a camera to a cabin trunk up the side of a mountain. A whole lamb cost 3/6d—a dozen eggs, 5d—a large basket of potatoes, 6d—a chicken, 4d. Thus the whole of our expedition up Mikeno, which took six days, including food and a retinue of twenty porters, cost rather less than it does today to take a girl out to dinner and a show in town . . . and, to my way of thinking, our way of spending the money was a whole lot more fun.

Presently, we left the shambas behind and came into what appeared to be a giant kitchen garden, which gradually developed into more normal forest. We found ourselves climbing slowly upwards along an elephant track. Very fresh droppings showed that the elephants themselves had only recently been doing the same thing and the porters kept up an intermittent shindy to prevent any kind of level crossing accident.

As we got further away from the native shambas, Gander and I went well ahead of the line of porters to be out of earshot of the disturbance, so that we could move along quietly and see what we could see. Presently various other game trails began to lead into ours and in a little while the muddy path showed evidence of a vast amount of animal traffic. Ours was quite evidently a main line track for most things—elephant, buffalo in quantity, bush pig, giant forest hog, leopard—big, middling and little, bush buck and countless other smaller fry. It was a most intriguing track and one that could prove completely ideal for our trip wires. The only trouble would be to sort out, from all these spoors muddled up together, the animal one wanted and to devise some scheme whereby a trip wire could select the right one. We decided then and there to try for permission to use this trail but we doubted whether we would be allowed to, as this part of the forest, and all Mikeno in fact, had doubly strict laws. We saw no lion spoor although the natives hold that there are plenty here—cheetah, too, apparently—and it was a bit early on in the climb to expect signs of gorillas although they have been known to come down this far.

It was lovely climbing up that forest trail—which presently got much steeper—watching where all the animals had been before us, and wondering how much time had elapsed between the passing of the leopard and the antelope. The "feeling" or "atmosphere," or what you will, of the forest is very difficult to describe. As we moved along quietly through that tangled world, where every shade of green imaginable is to be found, I seemed to undergo much the same emotions as I do when listening to great music. In both cases, with music and with the forest, it is there all round you, enveloping you, real and insistent—and yet not real and not insistent—and neither the one nor the other is really fully comprehensible. There are things, animals and melodies and chords, moving about there in the background and interwoven with the theme that have to rely on imagination rather than comprehension. And presently the whole thing becomes a background to one's thoughts . . . I found my thoughts wandering away, miles and miles away from the forests . . . way off to towns and other lesser ways of living—to friends, and friendships past and yet to come—to schemes—to things written, and to be written . . . I even found myself framing strange little bits of dialogue—dialogue between myself and . . . I don't know whom. . . . And then I would come all the way back to the Forests and the foot-

Cheetah

prints in the mud and to the mighty silent orchestra around one. . . . And there would be the great dark peak of Mikeno disappearing steeply into the clouds above us—and there, catching up with us, the long line of chattering porters and the little white lamb on the string.

That lamb was quite a study in itself—a study in the fallibility of fear. All the way along that trail, in such a strange world so far from home, the scent of leopard and of other things was ringing every alarm bell in its system—and it trotted along unwillingly, vociferously giving vent to all the secret and entirely incorrect fears it was having for its own well-being. Whenever we stopped, it nuzzled up to one's legs for protection against all the dangers in the wicked world around it. Yet it had nothing to fear from the leopard—only from us. I'm afraid I made friends with it and led it along on its string myself—and Gander made a variety of remarks about Hitlerian hypocrisy.

Eventually we went up through the bamboos and came to Kabara—a clearing in the Hagenia forest at about ten thousand five hundred feet. This is the wonderland which Carl Akeley called the most beautiful spot in all the world. He stayed there for ever and his grave is just over there in a corner of the clearing.

There is a small hut at Kabara which must have been made either by Martin Johnson or by the Akeley-Derscheid Expedition twelve years before, in 1927, and we took possession of it.

Njoki got us a meal and while we ate it, it rained quite heavily and then cleared up. Afterwards we wandered off into the forest taking photographs and looking rather fearfully at the peak above us. Binoculars made the view far less encouraging and showed there to be snow on the south face.

Later on Kasisi took a knife and quickly the lamb was no longer frightened of being so far from home. We sat around the

Wayside Halt. The lamb would nuzzle close whenever we stopped to rest.

fire in company with the porters who had a fine time carving up the carcass and arguing over who got which bit.

Of course, there are other things that I love, but that evening at Kabara I could not think of anything that I would sooner be doing than sitting round that fire on the grass. Black bodies were crowding all around. The chatter kept up with no apparent strain and every second sentence produced contagious chuckles—and now and again a kind of explosive laughter. Everything that either Gander or I said, or ate, or did, provided great interest and a good deal of amusement. And gradually the last of the light went and Mikeno and Karasimbi hid themselves in great black clouds, and it was almost, but not quite, raining—and the air was windless. Apart from the natives, whose noise we certainly did not grudge, the world was still and quiet and everything quite perfect.

I couldn't sleep at all that night—maybe there were so many things to think about, maybe the altitude after the plains, maybe just one of those nights one didn't sleep. In the morning Njoki came through with a magnificent breakfast of liver and kidney toast and made things better. During the night I had heard a great deal of scuffling going on and it turned out that the boys had speared an enormous rat in the hut—gray brown it was, with three inches of white at the end of its tail—and they had skinned it for us. After breakfast began the usual chaos and shouting that always ended up mysteriously with an orderly file of porters disappearing off into the forest bearing all our motley bundles on their heads.

We left Kabara at nine, and directly we had gone fifteen yards, a gang of large black birds, each one with a white collar, moved straight in and took possession of camp. They hopped around everywhere, eating the scraps—including the body of the rat. We felt like importing some of them and putting them on Hampstead Heath.

Almost immediately the path began to climb steeply upwards on the game trail—and continued to do so until we got to our second camp site. Spoor on this trail showed buffalo and antelope, including the little duiker, and leopard. All this was through Hagenia trees and very beautiful. Presently we spotted the wild celery that grows to a height of about six to eight feet. It looks like celery and it tastes like celery, but if you found some of it growing in your own garden, you would go straight back to the house and have a damn good look at the level in the whiskey bottle. This, however, is undoubtedly the gorilla's favourite food, and sure enough at this point we came across a considerable number of gorilla tracks and plenty of spoor leading across our trail—and we also found several of the nests they build for beds.

A little further up the giant heather began to appear in amongst the hagenias. This again is much the same story as the celery—only more so. One felt a little like an ant must feel in the highlands of Scotland, for this heather grows to a height of thirty feet.

It is just about at this point that the forest becomes purely fantastic and fairy-like—and incredibly more imaginative than anything Grimm, or Disney could ever create. You walk on carpets of moss and flowers amid surrealist trees and roots—and long trailers of Spanish moss hang from everywhere, and everything is weird and wonderful—and every color in the spectrum is used in the shadows and on the paths and each color ranges through every delicate shade imaginable.

Presently the trail came up and over the top of a hill and ran along the crest of a narrow, steep knife-edge whose sides fell sharply down for many hundreds of feet. Once over this, we came out into another new and wonderful world. The forest was left behind and in its place were fine uplands dotted about with giant heather and giant groundsel. From this ridge we could see well in all directions—all too well in the direction of Mount Mikeno.

We were, as it turned out, more than lucky with the weather because normally Mikeno behaves very badly to climbers—and there are comparatively few days in the year when it is possible to climb the final thousand feet. After many failures Mount Mikeno was eventually first conquered in August 1927 by a man called Père van Hoef. Since then there have been many more failures but it was climbed at four other times since that date. We had hoped, if we succeeded, to be the first Englishmen to get to the summit but we subsequently learned that a party from East Africa had succeeded the year before we were there.

We climbed along this ridge, which at times was as narrow as three to four feet, and eventually we came to the end where it ran straight to the foot of the final peak. Here, just over the right hand side of the ridge, to the south, we pitched camp on a small flat place where there was just room for the tent. Following a terrific, and final, jabberation the porters collected some wood for a fire and then left us to go back down to Kabara to sleep. They would not stay up at that altitude with us as they quite frankly said they didn't like it, and it was cold, and a stupid place to come to anyway. So off they went. Poor Njoki had no choice. Kasisi stayed with us as it was his job to do so. Chako and a Toto*, who never appeared to have any name, at all, also stayed—the one because he was supposed to know the final route and the second because, strangely enough, he wanted to come with us.

We were now at approximately twelve thousand seven hundred feet and it was cold. While Njoki and Kasisi were pitching the tent, I wandered up to the ridge a few yards away and suddenly heard a lion roar, not very far away and about level with me, in a nearby ravine. I called quickly to Gander

* *Young native "boy."*

and we heard it roar again. We were trying to spot it when clouds came rolling up and hid everything.

When there were not clouds about us, that camp site on the little ledge was a very impressive place. In front, at the end of a valley, stood Mount Visoke—a 13,000 ft. volcano. Half right was Mount Karasimbi—a 15,000 ft. volcano. Behind us, just over the ridge, two more volcanoes were in view—Nynagonga and Nyamlagira . . . and way down below us was Africa and countless square miles of mysterious forest. And finally, to the left, and almost falling on top of us, was Mount Mikeno. Clouds came and went between us and the mountains—over us and round us—and there were eagles in the sky. We watched these eagles as they seemed to hang motionless in the air—and when they, every now and again, went into a dive their wings made a screaming noise something like the sound of calico tearing.

Mikeno, or rather the bit still above us, was not a reassuring sight. It seemed there was a steep climb upwards for the next five hundred feet and then, above that, what appeared to be a sheer rock wall going straight up into the clouds for about another thousand feet—and for the life of me I couldn't see any reasonable way up the thing.

That night it was very cold. We slept in our bedding fully dressed and with the tent shut up as tight as it would go. Again I slept very badly and, at midnight or thereabouts, I heard something very big moving about outside, not far from the tent. When I did eventually get to sleep I woke Gander up by talking about something to do with twenty severed black ears lying on the ground. He told me to shut up or get back to my old subject of animals.

* * *

MT. MIKENO. The last 1,000 feet is steep.

# CHAPTER XVII: THE TOP

It was very cold getting out of bed the next morning. Frost was on the ground and our water supplies were frozen hard. I asked if anyone else had heard anything of my large animal moving about during the night and Kasisi said he had heard a "Ngagi"* not far from camp. We crouched around a small fire while we had breakfast—made final arrangements—sorted out all the necessary equipment, and finally departed just after 7 a.m. There was Kasisi, Chako, the nameless Toto, Gander and myself. Njoki, very wisely, stayed in camp.

The climb began steeply, up through fairly thickly massed lobelias, and gradually got steeper and steeper until, after about an hour, we were above most of the vegetation—far above tree level—and right at the foot of the rock face.

Here we found a steep scree gulley going up into the rock and becoming narrower as it got to the top. There was a difficult climb of some twenty feet at the top of this.

For the next two hours I had a lot of my "vertigo" and

* *Gorilla.*

GIANT LOBELIA. We worked our way up through a weird and curious world.

Gander had not a little of his "funk." We had brought a climbing rope with us but neither one of us was sufficiently confident of the other's capabilities to consider being linked to him and we argued that, even if both of us were going to kill ourselves, it was preferable that we should die separately and not in one glorious spectacular falling chain of bodies. So we gave the rope to Kasisi who slung it over his shoulder.

My diary now goes into minute description of each successive move we made on that final climb and calls back to my mind things and moments that I had hoped I had forgotten. I do not intend to inflict the reader or myself (for two quite different reasons) with all this. Suffice it to say that it wasn't easy, and, in a spirit of great generosity, that to a real, hard-boiled, insensitive mountaineer it wouldn't have been difficult.

I have to admit, however, that I was scared. It wasn't vertigo *all* the time. . . . I was, in fact, generally apprehensive all the way up. The trouble was that it wasn't only steep, hellish steep, and even vertical in places, but all the rock was friable and such hand and foot holds as they were were liable to crumble and break away. And everything was sodden and wet and largely covered with great clumps of thick green spongy moss which gave no hold at all, and broke away and went tumbling off into nowhere. And on the steep slopes in between the rock faces there were great grass tussocks that were miserably insecure, and everything one touched was slimy and wet and slippery.

We struggled up somehow. Sometimes we were climbing—more or less properly—and sometimes we were merely swarming up on our bellies, relying more on surface friction than on any firm hold or anything else.—and all the time Africa was a hell of a long way down below—straight below. At one time or another each one of us got stuck, but mutual admiration methods got us unstuck on each occasion. Near the top we came into snow. It wasn't really snow as I know it—it was

Climbing. All hand and foot holds tended to crumble and give way.

Mikeno Crater. Extinct—but difficult going.

rather masses of small hailstones frozen together which gave no security at all and merely rattled off down the mountain when touched.

But eventually we got to the top of the cliff and came up to the safe top slopes. From here there was still a steepish climb to the top lava ridge. On one side of this ridge there was a sheer precipice for a short while, but after this, with a slight twist, it developed into a gently rising slope that ended in the summit.

On the very top, at 14,642 feet, one stood on black dust and lava blocks in a space about twenty-five feet across with more or less sheer drops on three sides. The rocks and the ground were quite noticeably warm and down on the north-west side there was a large lava plateau from which a little steam was rising.

We were very lucky with the weather as we had sunshine until we were only one hundred feet from the top. I can well understand how Mikeno quickly becomes unclimbable in the bad weather it most often has. In cloud and rain, which are usual for more than three hundred days of the year, we certainly would not have got anywhere at all. However, we got up—and it was gratifying to think that Albert, King of the Belgians, who was no mean climber, had failed.

We sat for about twenty minutes on the summit in the clouds. We smoked a cigarette and ate some chocolate and I, if I may be so ordinary, would like to record that I spent my highest penny yet. On the summit, under the remains of a cairn that had been blasted by lightning, we found a broken bottle which had contained a paper giving the names of previous parties—but the paper was charred and unreadable. We did however find a film spool case under some rocks which gave us the names of the last party up. We wrote out our names and the times and dates on a sheet of paper and put it into a Leica cassette and left it with theirs.

14,700 FEET. We sat around for twenty minutes on the very summit in the clouds, and smoked a cigarette.

Coming down, the clouds and mist fortunately hid the more frightening drops below one—but it was far colder and we both suffered from finger trouble.

When we got down to the bottom of the cliff again Chako and Kasisi went into a wild and impromptu dance of celebration. The little nameless Toto, however, was far too cold and bothered about everything to catch the real spirit of the thing. A little lower down we were within sight and earshot of camp, and there we could see and hear the party of porters who had come back to fetch us and our belongings. A series of yells passed between us and camp, and when Gander and I could get a word in we shouted down, "Make tea. . . . Take down the tent . . . we're going to Kabara." This was evidently favourable information to those down below because that tent came down quicker than if they had cut the guy ropes. And then began a mad rush and slither and run and jump down through the lobelias back to camp.

And there we were greeted with a terrific jabberation of congratulation—particularly from Njoki who was convinced he had seen the last of us that morning. After we had had a cup of hot tea we set off back down the game trail to Kabara, and my legs just got me there.

The next day, after a long session following up gorillas, we went on down to Kibumba and it was over—and from then on I enjoyed looking up at Mikeno with its rocky peak disappearing up into the clouds.

* * *

# CHAPTER XVIII: THE SOLUTION

It was in the Tchibinda Hills that we first saw pygmies in, if I may misadapt a current phrase, a big way. We had come across them individually here and there in the forests elsewhere, but at Tchibinda we got to know them better as we employed them to help with our plans. The real out-and-out pygmy lives in the Ituri Forest, where we were planning to go later on to get pictures of the okapi. Those plans, however, never came to fruition because by this date "Peace in our time" was undergoing pretty severe revision, and the sickle was being sharpened for September 1939.

I'm afraid that in those days of June, July, and August of that same year (of no grace at all) we somehow didn't find much time for keeping abreast of international politics. There was so much of interest to distract one from the monotony of hearing Hitler make his daily claim that this or that or the other was positively his very *latest* territorial ambition—and that his patience was exhausted—and all that. . . . We hadn't, of course, the same opportunity for following the news as the gentlemen in England, then well and truly abed. We hadn't

GORILLA COUNTRY. Looking down on the forests of Mikeno's slopes. We could see one tent on a ridge below us.

got the *Daily Express* or the *Mail* or the *Herald* or any evening papers—and dear old Auntie *Times*, when she arrived, panting and rather scandalised, at Goma, was as up-to-date as the things you find in a dentist's waiting room. We hadn't a radio, and the little hostel at Goma, even for the short periods when we were there, only provided something that it called a radio.

When any event of import took place in Europe, news of it would arrive out in the Congo through the usual mysterious channels of "Have you heard . . . ?" If it was a good piece of news, it arrived in the Congo far better—and if a bad piece of news, infinitely worse. It was always much the same story as the old one of the four years' war where a message starts out from headquarters as "Send reinforcements, we are going to advance," and which arrived at its destination in the form of "Send three and fourpence, we are going to a dance." On top of this, the news that was filtering through from Europe was so fantastic at its very source that we never could tell whether the African rumour had been at it or not.

So I regret to say we rather tended to the attitude of never troubling trouble until trouble troubled us, and of getting on with the job we had in hand—and we had innocently made plans which would have carried us well over into 1940.

If I remember aright, the first time I ever saw a pygmy was when I was on my own in the middle of the forest. There were times when we decided to go off separately and alone, to do the seven, eight, or even twelve and fifteen mile round of the camera traps, just for the fun and adventure of being all on one's own in the forest. On this particular occasion I was stalking around as quietly as I could, inspecting this and repairing that, and telling myself that I wasn't scared of anything at all—when suddenly I found that I was scared—badly scared. I had looked up from the job I was doing on a camera and there, standing in front of me, about five or six yards away and half hidden in the thick foliage, was a tiny little black man, wizened and ugly, practically naked, and carrying a large bow and arrow. He was watching me intently. I stood up and looked at him. He was, as I said, an ugly little man and he had no expression at all on his face. The next moment a couple of large dogs, with very definite unpleasant expressions on their faces, came stiffly up to me with hackles raised and sniffed around my legs and ankles registering intense disapproval. I tried my best at a nonchalant greeting in Swahili—as though it was for me a common occurrence meeting ugly little men like him in the forests. It sounded hollow even to me, and there was no response and no movement. I tried in French and then in English and in German. . . . I must say that hearing myself saying "*Bon jour*" suddenly sounded peculiar—and then the ugly little man just wasn't there any more. . . . I never heard him come and I never heard him go—one minute he was there, looking at me, and the next, he wasn't.

That is much how they are, the pygmies. The forest is their home and they know it as well as, if not better than, you or I know Main Street of our own home towns. They never on any single occasion touched a black cotton trip wire. In some mysterious fashion they would suddenly stop a few yards away from where a cotton was stretched and then make a sizeable detour round through the forest before rejoining the trail on the far side. One of them would snap off a twig at the side of the path and that would be sufficient warning for any later passers-by. . . . Such a sign, amid all the tangle of the forest, was to a pygmy as obvious as traffic lights are to the motorist.

The Belgian Administration leaves the pygmies very much to themselves—which, on the whole, is very sensible of it, for if one had to do anything about the pygmies, I'm hanged if I would know where to begin. It would be like trying to collect mercury in a huge mountainous hairbrush. They are respected as individuals and are even granted certain privileges—for instance, they are the only natives allowed to hunt in the Reserve —and the only ones allowed to light fires.

The pygmies we had to deal with were mostly Batwa, or semi-Pygmy—a type that is slightly larger than the pygmies from the Ituri Forest. In the Tchibinda hills we found him to be an independent little number. He would do certain things if he wanted to, but if he didn't he wouldn't—and he appeared to take orders from no one. He slips in and out of the shadows of the forest as he will, and, like the nursery rhyme about the cat, "if you don't hurt him he'll do you no harm."

The only harm the pygmies did to me was indirect. . . . They live in an almost completely primitive state and they have many cunning methods of trapping game. Among these, a more ordinary method is the one of digging deep holes at unexpected places along the game trails—setting sharp spikes points upwards at the bottom of the holes, and then concealing the whole thing with brushwood and foliage. The elephant or the buffalo or the antelope comes along, thinking of this and that, steps on a piece of ground that isn't there, and down he goes on to the spikes. It works very well. I know, because I did it myself.

We were coming more and more to the conclusion that to take flashlight pictures of gorillas by the methods we had used on other animals was not a feasible proposition. There was always the possibility that blind chance would bring an unexpected reward and that a camera set at ten or eleven thousand feet above sea level for some more normal animal might indeed bag a gorilla—but there were so many things that might go wrong with the camera or the trip or the mechanism that even such a chance offering might well be missed by some technical hitch. In any case we did not approve of blind chance—we wanted somehow to make the thing as near a certainty as possible.

We had considered every possibility and almost every impossibility. The only hope seemed to be to attract the gorilla

UPLAND FANTASY

in some way to some given spot which we could prepare beforehand. We had even considered the impossibility of clearing a large area of the forest of wild celery, leaving only one big bunch of it (bristling with flash bulbs and black cotton) growing at a suitable spot. We had also thought of tempting him with alluring clumps of bananas at unexpected places. This worked well with chimpanzees on the volcano Hehu. Some people held it would work with gorillas and some were emphatic that it would interest them not at all. For one reason or another we never had time to try out this theory, but I myself do not believe it would have worked.

We thought of portable gramophones with records of gorilla sounds and of putting ourselves in some well protected hide from which would emerge a selection of these sounds in the hope that the gorillas in the forests would become curious to see what was going on. And finally we tried hard not to think of the possibility of advancing on the gorilla armed only with cameras, in the hope that the blinding flash of the bulbs would turn a charge and scare the animal away. Risky as this would undoubtedly have been, I believe that it might have worked. From observation of the reactions of other animals to the light of the flash bulbs we had good reason to believe that even a gorilla would turn—but still . . .

So in the end we decided that some new method would have to be devised.

We found from experiment that if we used all twenty cameras in a line, allowing for natural obstacles such as big trees through which a gorilla could not pass, we could achieve a "frontage" of trip wires of some forty to fifty yards. The next thing to do was to discover some place in the gorilla forest where there was a narrow bottleneck or some narrowing down of the confines of the forests to approximately this distance. If we could find such a place, through which the gorillas were normally accustomed to pass in order to get from one feeding ground to another, then things would begin to look brighter. We would then be able to put up our Siegfried Line in peace and at our leisure, when no gorillas were about, and make sufficient clearance of the undergrowth to allow each camera its requisite "field of vision" and then . . . well, then the plan was, not so much to *drive* the gorillas up to the line as to *persuade* them, by one means and another, to transfer from one feeding area to another by way of the bottleneck.

On paper it was fine. In practice it was obvious that we should want considerable assistance, first to discover the gorillas, second to discover the place, and third to help us to persuade the gorillas from one area to another. There was only one source to which we could go for the knowledge we required and the assistance that was necessary, and that was, the pygmies.

The Belgians in the Tchibinda area were helpfulness itself. After we had been taken round to various places and had seen plenty of evidence of gorillas, a meeting with the pygmy chief was arranged for nine o'clock one morning at the edge of the forest.

* * *

# CHAPTER XIX: LITTLE AND BIG

We arrived at our rendezvous with the pygmy chief punctually at nine o'clock, accompanied by an excellent young Dutchman called Van Leeuwen. He had been very kindly lent to us as interpreter from the National Institute for the Scientific Study of Agriculture (called "L'Ineac") and as he had five languages perfectly at his command, my poor tortuous French had a rest for a change.

At about eleven in the morning the pygmy chief, whose name was Kasalo, accompanied by his son, came sauntering out of the forest and sat down. They seemed to blink rather a lot in the sunlight after the dark shadows of the forests. At various intervals, other lesser pygmies came wandering out and joined the meeting to see what it was all about, until presently there were about fifteen to twenty of them sitting around on the grass in front of us.

This was the first time that we had seen the little men in any kind of quantity. Their clothing consisted of a piece of string slung low round the hips, with any old scrap of odd cloth pulled up between the legs, passed under the string, and left to dangle for a few inches fore and aft in a modest,

WATUSSI CELEBRATION. The orchestra.

Watussi Celebration. Dancers.

but often unsuccessful attempt to hide the pygmy machinery. Each carried a spear, and each one was uglier than the one beside him.

It was also the first time Njoki had seen them, and they had the effect on him of making him roar with laughter—which was very embarrassing all round and he had to be sent away to sit in the car.

The conversations opened with the help of two interpreters. We put our questions to the Dutchman. The Dutchman passed them on to a local native who spoke both Swahili and pygmy language. The native passed on the questions to Kasala, the chief pygmy, who then consulted the gang. Answers had to come back all through the same chain. It must have been about as confusing as an international conference.

And so began a meeting which lasted for the best part of two full days—during which time we had to try to pound into the pygmy mind the manifold subtleties and complications of our Rube Goldberg photographic schemes, and to try to get, for the umpteenth time, definite answers to questions about the habits of gorillas—and finally, to get them to agree to help us. The Dutchman was quite magnificent, and infinitely patient. He went slowly at each problem or explanation and repeated each point over time and again before even demanding an answer. The pygmies sat around and listened, and their expressions were more than intriguing to watch. Sometimes they would burst out laughing at the things we wanted to know —"The white man has something in his head which we do not understand"—(This later became quite a catch phrase between Gander and myself.) The general attitude, however, was one of fortunate tolerance for people who apparently liked to go about simple tasks in the most complicated manner—and, bit by bit, ever so "pole-pole,"* answers began to come forth. . . .

* *Gently.*

At one point in the conversations interest clearly began to flag a little. One of the lesser pygmies had a small musical instrument in his lap, a hollowed-out box affair with small strips of metal set across a bar on top which, if I remember right, is called a "Likembe." He began absent-mindedly to pluck away at this instrument, and presently to build up the rhythm. Heads began to wag and legs to twitch. One or two of the others got up and began to dance—and within two minutes we and our schemes were forgotten, and the whole bunch, Chief Kasalo and all, were leaping around in a wild and impromptu jive session.

After a bit they all sat down again—somebody said "Next question, please," and everybody felt a lot better.

It is possible that some of these international conferences might benefit from taking a leaf out of the pygmy book. I would dearly love to see this method practised in the House of Commons, where sometimes the white man has ideas in his head that even the white man cannot understand.

But those conversations were, in the end, highly rewarding. The pygmies eventually got the idea and were evidently rather intrigued by it, as they definitely agreed to play. It was finally arranged that they would go off, make a full report on the present whereabouts of the majority of the gorillas, find a suitable place, if possible, for the line of cameras, and finally help us in the matter of persuading the gorillas through the trip-wires. All of this would naturally take time, and it was agreed that we were to go off and complete another task on the Kabara game trail and elsewhere, and return with all the equipment in two to three weeks' time.

Well . . . there it was . . . that was the plan . . . and, although there were still plenty of snags, I think in the end we could have made it work. But, as I have hinted at already, we never got back to try it out . . . the sands ran out on September the third.

Watussi Cattle. Beasts with an incredible spread of horns.

CEREMONIAL. Each owner would dance around the beast that had the finest head.

But meeting the pygmies had been wonderfully interesting. They were small enough for us not to be reduced, as one African writer was, to standing on a box beside them to make an impressive photograph. Generally speaking, the young ones are vastly more intelligent than the adults. They reach what is politely known as "that certain age" just about when they celebrate their tenth birthday, and from then on they do themselves pretty proud along the road to ruin. Pombe, or native banana beer, consumed in large quantities does not lead to brightness. Tobacco, wood ash, or practically anything that will smoulder, smoked incessantly, helps things along—and finally, as soon as he is able (which is practically from the age of ten onwards) a young pygmy is hard to beat at sowing his fair share of wild oats. So, by the age of twenty he looks far older than his years and the intellect has rather taken a back seat.

He is small and he is ugly, and, in his stance and squat and shape of skull, his thin lips and his more developed *système pileux,* he differs a lot from the remainder of the African Tribes. His women folk are uglier still. They use some mysterious herbal contraceptive, but they are nevertheless pretty fertile, and the infant mortality is on the high side. The pygmies suffer from a foot disease called "pion" and occasionally, of all things, from elephantiasis. They are wonderful hunters and trackers in the forests. So far as I could make out, none of those whom we met was a Christian and they all appear to be scared of ghosts. During periods of full moon, they are likely to do away with sleeping and to dance whole nights through to keep the ghosts at bay.

They are, however, quite pleasant little people and, as is the case with most African natives, laughter comes easily. They like payment for services rendered and, wherever possible, for services not rendered. Money isn't much use to them, but, if they like you, they will do a lot for salt, matches and tobacco.

It always seemed to me slightly like reading one of the more ambitious and less authentic adventure stories to find that only a few miles away from the miniature men of the forests, one could find a race of men most of whom are well over seven foot tall. To travel from the Ituri Forest to Ruanda Urundi you can go from three foot eleven to better than seven feet. Much has already been written about the Watussi Tribe, who are originally of Nilotic descent. I was fortunate enough to go down to Kigale in Ruanda Urundi at a time when the Watussi were celebrating something or other by holding a dance which went on solidly for two days and two nights. I did not stay that long myself for I wore myself to a shred just watching them dance for an afternoon.

The Watussi, apart from the difference of height, is the complete opposite of the pygmy. He dresses in long flowing white robes, carries himself with considerable dignity and has a way of making one feel, as well as look, very small indeed. He is the aristocrat—tall and dark and handsome—and intelligent as well. He lets himself go however in his style of hairdressing—mowing as it were, great winding fairways down through the woolly rough—giving the impression that some lunatic barber had got loose on a customer with a pair of electric clippers. And when he dances he most certainly lets himself go. Even taking pictures at a 500th of a second I often failed miserably to stop the frenzied movement. Hour after hour they leaped and stamped, pounding bare feet on mud—dancing and pounding—pounding and chanting—chanting and yelling—until the whole world contained nothing else than the ceaseless, hypnotic, maddening and yet entrancing rhythm of Africa.

My enthusiasm for pictures took me into the arena with them in order to get close-ups of the violent and intoxicating activity. For my pains I got hit over the head by a whirling spear.

WATUSSI PRINCESS. I wasn't supposed to take this picture—but I don't think she minded.

Half way through the afternoon the arena was cleared for the chief Watussi sport—namely high jumping. With my own eyes I saw a man clear the bar at seven feet, two inches. . . . Well . . . you say . . . why don't the Watussi win the world championship? Because there is a little matter of the take-off and the Amateur Athletic Association Rules. Just in front of the high-jump itself, they dig a small hole in the ground and in this they firmly plant a small boulder which sticks some four inches up above the ground. In jumping, with a straight run at the bar, one bare foot goes on to this boulder and then up and over the bar they go . . . and it has a kind of springboard effect of converting horizontal movement into vertical. This, according to A.A.A. rules, is cheating, and without it the Watussi cannot jump so very high. As a performance, however, it is definitely impressive, and in order to complicate the issue they seem to insist on jumping in their long flowing white robes—which can scarcely help.

They dearly love their high jumping. Every village has its competitions and its champions—and every year there is an all-Watussi championship—to which all the people swarm. In all Africa it is unique, and harmless, and pleasing, rather like cricket in England.

So much for the little and the big. I dare say they have forgotten about me—but I haven't forgotten about them. I wish I was back there among them now where pens and newspapers and telephones and radios have no place at all.

* * *

# CHAPTER XX: THE RADIO

During the time we were waiting for the Tchibinda plans to take shape, while the Pygmies were doing their side of the arrangement, we decided to go back to Mikeno and to try to get permission to use the Kabara track—that lovely and promising game-trail that we had followed on the way up the mountain.

There was not much time left now before the good weather we had been having would break, and, when we called in at Costermansville and Goma, there were the wildest rumors from the European scene. So we decided for this short period to split up into two parties again, in order to cover as much ground as possible and to get as many results as we could. . . . We tossed up to see who should have the Kabara track, if permits were forthcoming, and I must have won, for I got it.

Colonel Hoier straight away gave us the necessary permission and very kindly allowed us the use of his little hut which he had built right at the point where the track left the native shambas and entered the forests on its long winding journey up Mikeno via Kabara. He used this hut much as a

primitive kind of hunting lodge when he went out on his periodic safaris to inspect that portion of his huge domain—and that is precisely what I did with it, too.

I stayed there, Kibumba, it was called, for some ten days and it was, I suppose, a period during which I came as near to absolute contentment as I ever have in my life. I wrote home a fairly long letter giving a description of that place—and the letter was kept. I would like, if I may, to take an extract from that letter instead of writing a fresh description.

"I am," I wrote, "like Greta Garbo, all alone. Gander has gone off to other parts on other photographic quests. I am here with half the cameras to try for elephant and buffalo, with the off-chance of gorilla thrown in. Colonel Hoier, the chief game Warden of the whole Reserve, has lent me the place, Kibumba, for as long as I care to use it. So I now have a wonderful little wooden house of my own with a stove and a chimney and a table and a few chairs, and other rather primitive odds and ends, all to myself. It is like something straight out of a fairy tale and I wish I could describe how fascinating it is and how happy I am to be here.

When I say I am alone I am not counting the natives, the various boys employed and paid by us and the many locals who work their own cultivated area round about and who seem to have attached themselves to our retinue.

There are four rooms in my little house. I have a sitting-room-cum-dining-room which I seem to share with several hens that Njoki has bought (or come by in some other means). I have a bedroom all to myself, and a camp bed. On the other side of the sitting room there is a mysterious room in which several natives live and from whence, in some peculiar fashion, is produced beautiful fresh milk and butter. I wouldn't put it beyond Njoki to have a cow in there.

Beyond that again is a foggy, steamy place that is the kitchen. Out of this room, in the center of the floor of which a log fire permanently burns, come roast lamb and piping hot soup and various unidentifiable "Njoki Specialties"—all to the ceaseless rhythm of African music from African instruments. Always, crouched down somewhere in the dark corners below the smoke from the fire, there are one or two dark shining bodies plucking away at the metal bars of their likembes. Always the tune appears to be the same. At first I didn't know how I was going to put up with it—that maddening, insistent, endless rhythmical plucking that produced sounds like the birthpangs of a modern melody that couldn't somehow quite get born—and now I can't do without it. If it stops, I shout—and it goes on again. . . .

Outside, there is a garden. It isn't a garden such as you have at home. It is a wild, tangled place where flowers and vegetables vie with one another side by side. It produces vegetables of all sorts and a mass of exotic flowers grow haphazardly here and there. In front of the windows are tall white lilies as big as trumpets, and to get in and out of the door you have to fight your way through roses. Just back of the hut is a strawberry bed, the middle of which is an elephant track. Between the hut and that important place the Auntie, which of course is outside and very, very primitive, there is leopard spoor fresh from last night. Just over there is the forest—a great green wall of trees, and all around there is of course the inevitable dramatic back-cloth of volcanoes—the highest peaks of which, at the moment, are snow-capped. In the daytime there is sunshine and at night-time, the fires of Nynagonga glow brightly against the sky—and at any time in the twenty four hours there are violent, quick thunderstorms with heavy downpours and startling lightning effects.

If the hut is small, the staff is large. Njoki is major-domo. Then there is Kasisi, who is the Park Policeman, and who is shortly to go to jail for bribery. Then there is a big cheerful black chap, who wears a kind of bath towel round his middle,

Njoki's Department. He could always be relied upon to come through with something hot.

Ugly Little Man. He made a large bow and arrow.

and whom I call Sanatogen because his name sounds something like that and because he looks like the advertisements. Then there is Njoki's kitchen Toto, our gentleman's personal gentleman, so to speak. . . . Then another Toto, who crouches in the corner of my room and puts wood in the stove every now and again—and puffs and puffs into the innards of the contraption and succeeds in blowing clouds of smoke out into the room. Another to get wood. Another to get water. Innumerable others who keep popping up out of nowhere and grin and act as porters. There are lots to do this and that and the other, and always some left over to stand and stare and watch the B'wana cleaning his teeth or writing his letters. They come and go much as they like, in and out, and I like them coming and going, as they amuse me as much as I amuse them—and they pick up all the cigarette ends.

Within a radius of some five to seven miles I have placed out and set ten camera traps, and my days are spent out there in the forests. In the evenings, I keep the necessary records and diary and do various repairs—and just sit and look around me in a contented kind of way and listen to that maddeningly entrancing rhythm that comes from the kitchen. Within the same radius as my cameras are some two to three hundred elephant—and some of these are forever causing alarms and excursions among the natives by wandering into the garden outside.

I have a tame pygmy with me who looks like a cross between Solomon and a gorilla. He is making me a large bow and arrow.

I am not all that handsome myself now. The nearest barber being about three hundred miles away, if not more, I have cut my own hair. I went through a variety of styles to see the effects and this has inevitably ended up with a Teutonic quarter-inch crop. My beard on the other hand is in a fine state of wild abandon and is rivaling the tangled garden outside. I have lived and slept in the same clothes now for at least the past month . . . and I am very happy . . . "

That is what I wrote when I was on the spot. If I was flippant in places—well, I was flippant—and I expect by now that the reader has discovered that that is what is wrong with everything I write. . . . I cannot keep flippancy out somehow. But it was a time of utter contentment, of satisfying adventure by day in the forests and of complete peace of mind in the evenings. . . . Easy to remember, but difficult, these days, to recapture.

There was a rough, bumpy track that connected my little hut to the main Goma-Rutshuru road. One day, when I was way off in the forest down below the road, I met a native who said that there was a white man waiting for me back in camp. The natives were always, in some mysterious fashion, at least one jump ahead of us in the way of local news, and when I got back there surely enough, of all things to see leaning up against the hut, was a bicycle. And inside the hut I found a Canadian —a young fellow whose name turned out to be Leitch. He was having tire trouble on the volcanic road surfaces, and hearing that there was an Englishman up the track, he had decided to come and call and maybe get assistance.

I asked him where he had come from and how he had got here. His answer was that he had bicycled here—via England, France, most of Europe, Yugo-Slavia, Albania, Greece, Turkey, Palestine, Egypt—all the way down to Nairobi, and then across the way that we had come.

We spent an excellent evening together and he, naturally, had many an interesting story to tell. He was a student, studying mining engineering, and primarily interested in diamonds. He was proposing to return to Canada via South Africa, India, Burma, Dutch East Indies, Australia and the Pacific islands—all by bicycle. His journey so far, from Canada to

Busily scratching one hind leg with the other.

the Congo had cost him approximately eighteen pounds. I often wonder how far he got before September came.

I drove him and his punctured bicycle into Goma and returned home. When I got back Njoki was waiting for me, bursting with curiosity. He wanted to know all about the B'wana with the bicycle. I did my best. I got most of it across —but I became very involved geographically in the later stages.

"White man come from America, B'wana?"

"Yes, Njoki." (Near enough, I thought.)

"By bicycle, B'wana?"

"No, Njoki."

"Why not, B'wana?"

"Very many waters, Njoki."

"Has B'wana been to America?"

"Yes, Njoki."

"By car, B'wana?"

"No, Njoki."

"Why not, B'wana?".

"Very many waters, Njoki."

"Water bad very."

"Yes, Njoki, water bad very."

"Where is America, B'wana?"

"Very many miles, Njoki, and . . . er . . . over there . . . "

Following all this we got all mixed up with Nairobi and Johannesburg and the points of the compass, and then Kasisi and one or two others came in—so we had it all over again. I got badly off the tracks trying to explain about diamonds.

"Does the white man go after animals, B'wana?"

"No, Kasisi, after little stones."

"The B'wana with the bicycle goes after little stones?"

"Yes, Kasisi."

"What the hell for?" (in so many words)

"Little stones—lots of francs, Kasisi."

And so on for a very long time, until eventually, I told them all to go away and come back again at seven o'clock in the morning.

I made many trips up into the forest toward Kabara, and also down into the forest way below camp and on the far side of the road—where there was a lot of game—and sometimes, when I went down there, if I was going to be late, I took the car and drove back in the dark. There was hardly one time when I made that drive by night when I did not have some kind of encounter with elephants on the road. It was always exciting, sometimes dangerous . . . and occasionally comic.

I remember one evening particularly when I was driving back fairly late and came to a place where I had set two camera traps not thirty yards off the road in the forest. I slowed the car down to a walking pace and was debating whether I dared sneak in there in the dark to see if either trap had caught anything during the evening—when suddenly I saw a bright flash and the next thing was an elephant charging through the forest towards me. He came out of the bushes on the right hand side of the road right out in front of the car. There, less than fifteen yards off in the full glare of the headlights, he came to a slithering halt in a cloud of dust. Never have I seen a more startled elephant. He stood facing the headlights for one breathless moment—made some desperate sort of gesture with his trunk as if to say, "God! . . . more lights! . . . What's come over the old place . . . " and then he wheeled and charged off through the undergrowth on the left hand side of the road and was gone, all elephantine dignity patently thrown to the four winds.

My tame pygmy came through with a fine bow and arrow and the next thing was, of course, that nobody in camp would leave me in peace until I had shown how well the white man could shoot. Eventually, I went out reluctantly behind the hut, followed by all the gang. I drew the bow, aimed vaguely in the direction of a large tree, shut my eyes and let go. When I

"God!—More lights? What's come over the old place?"

opened them the arrow was quivering in a small branch half way up the tree and the audience was applauding wildly.

I was all for letting it go at that, but no, B'wana had to shoot another. . . . I repeated the process, closed my eyes again and let fly. This time there was a stony silence. . . . When I opened my eyes I couldn't for a moment see the arrow anywhere. And then, fortunately, I spotted it—it was deeply embedded two inches away from the first arrow in the same small branch.

I turned silently and went back into the hut followed by wide-eyed stares of amazement. My reputation was made—and nothing on God's earth would ever make me shoot my bow and arrow again.

I loved that time I had by myself at Kibumba—but I was glad when Gander came back and joined me. He had not had much success with his cameras—and we sat up practically all through the first night sharing the hundred and one things we had to discuss. One way and another I had had several adventures with my elephants and I was not altogether surprised to have Gander report in the morning that I had been at it again in my sleep. . . . This time it was, "Oh dear, it's another elephant. . . . There's an elephant down there on the right . . ."

We made final plans to start off after the gorillas in a few days' time, and we bought all the necessary stores for the trip in Goma—and meanwhile we had a final fling together at the Kabara track with all twenty cameras.

It was a day or two before we were due to leave that we went down and drove to Romangabo as a gesture to say au revoir to Colonel Hoier and to ask a few final questions before we left. We were in tremendous form as we marched up to his little wooden house and rattled a tattoo on the door.

The moment he opened the door to us we knew something was wrong. He had a face as long as a boot.

"Have you heard?"

"No. What?"

"It's war."

"Oh God," we said. "Between whom now?"

"England and Germany."

"Oh God . . . "

And then, with leaden hearts, we went inside—and later we crouched around the Colonel's radio which every now and again was just audible. And when the news came on there was a recording of a speech being relayed. It was a still small voice crying into the wilderness . . . we could just catch the salient points, "I am a man of peace . . . a state of war has been declared to-day between this country and Germany . . . "

I forget the exact words—And with blinding, awful suddenness, the Age of Collective Obscurity was on.

* * *

# CHAPTER XXI: FINALE

The whole atmosphere changed at once. The magic of the moment vanished and the great dark cloud of the near-future came rolling up and enveloped us, and freedom and fun were obscured and lost to view. It was a very different pair that left Romangabo that night to drive back to Kibumba.

The next morning we left everything where it stood in camp and out in the forests, and drove the three hundred odd miles to Kabale in Uganda—to get in touch with a proper radio and to hear the full story—and finally to decide on the next move.

On arrival at Kabale that evening the first thing we saw was a cricket match—close cropped green turf, white flannels, tea and lemonade under the shady trees—incredibly English looking, incredibly peaceful, incredibly unruffled—it reminded us of Francis Drake and the game of bowls. But the radio at the hotel filled in all the sinister gaps and we learned the full story.

A day later we drove back again across the Kinaber Pass, with no eyes for the scenery and no thoughts for the adventures that lay behind the walls of the forests, back to Kibumba;

and then we set about packing up the whole safari. It took us a full day to collect all the cameras out of the forests. During our absence the weather had broken and the skies were looking and behaving much as we felt, and the forest was a steamy sea of mud. The cameras were soaked and dripping, and nearly all the trip-wires were broken.

Then we collected all the boys together and paid them off. It was a melancholy performance—they couldn't understand what had suddenly happened, and we were loath to explain that the white men were doing exactly what the white men had spent so long telling the black men that they must not do, fight among themselves. . . . The salaries due to them seemed such pitifully small sums to be paying them for all the loyalty they had given us. We asked each one, Sebihaza, Rubanza, Magura, Muhima, Sendoki, Kiemba, all down the line, what he would like in the way of "Baksheesh," and each time we did this a pair of great black eyes would roll around until they came to rest on the pile of expended flash-bulbs that lay in a corner of the hut. And so, besides some extra money, each one of them got one or two used flash-bulbs with a reminder not to bash them about. Later, when they and their families gathered to see us off, we saw that their womenfolk were proudly wearing these flash-bulbs—some of them in the oddest places.

I still have a sharply vivid and poignant memory of Kasisi and Sanatogen, and one or two others, running down the track after the car as we left.

All petrol had suddenly vanished out of the Congo. We had to borrow from Colonel Hoier's private stock to get away at all—and, all the way out of the Congo and all across Africa, we had to switch off and coast down all the hills in order to make sure of getting to the next supply point.

At Kampala we walked, forgetful of our ragged and shaggy appearance, bearded and dirty, straight into the big hotel. It

THE END. It is difficult to make an attractive picture of the wrong end of a hippo.

was a Sunday afternoon and all the Kampala world and its wife was in the lounge for the dreary social ritual of afternoon tea. We were brought back to our senses, and to the full realization of what we looked like to civilized eyes, by the sudden deathly hush that descended on the lounge the moment we entered. And then, from one of the tables, a voice said clearly, "Good God . . . Don't tell me the Russians are in already . . ."

Gander got a job in Nairobi with Force Headquarters—and I got dysentery. As soon as I was well enough, I decided to head for England, Home and Duty—and to do whatever it was that England expected. . . . I travelled back down the whole length of the Nile from Lake Kioga to Cairo—and, in the end, I never got to England. . . . I stayed in the Middle East. . . . But all that is another story.

Gander and I met once again in 1940 in Jerusalem. After that we didn't meet any more.

I only wish that it were possible to go back once more, with him, to those dark fantastic forests and to finish off the job we started, and shared, so happily together.

I can almost see him now, sitting here and reading these pages I have written, and looking up at me with that funny characteristic smile, half mischievous and half amused, and saying, ". . . Not bad, Jimmy. Not good—but not bad. A little inaccurate in places, perhaps, but then it all happened a long time ago. . . . But I do hate all those dots you will insist on using. . . ."

He would, as I said at the beginning, have done it much better.

THE END.

London, November 1945.

# ACKNOWLEDGMENTS

Our thanks are due—long overdue in fact—to the following people, whose hospitality, help, kindness and advice, were very much appreciated:—

M. Jean Wittouck, of Brussels.

Professor E. van Straelen, Natural History Museum, Brussels.

Colonel Hoier, Chief Game Warden, Park National Albert.

Commandant Hubert, Game Warden, Ruindi Camp.

Colonel Ritchie, Chief Game Warden, Kenya.

Victor Mardon, of Eburru, Kenya.

Mr. and Mrs. Mervyn Rae, and Eric and Billy, of Kinangop Escarpment.

"Weary" Wood, of Kodak's, Nairobi.

Rachael and Jim Richards, of Nairobi.

The Proprietors of the Bell Inn, Naivasha.

Mr. G. A. Heath, Game Warden, Naivasha.

Zacchy Craus.

Mr. Stradio, Provincial Administrator, Costermansville.

Mr. Stoffels, of L'Ineac, Mulungu.

Mr. and Mrs. H. V. van Leeuwen, of L'Ineac, Mulungu.

The Proprietors of the Hotel des Volcans, Goma.

The Bishop of Uganda and Mrs. Stuart.

The White Fathers of Lulengu Mission.

Mr. Bormans, Game Warden, Costermansville.

And to many others whose names, in view of the lapse of time, I either cannot remember or find in my records. I hope they will forgive me.